# There's a New Day Coming!

## A survey of endtime events

## Herbert Vander Lugt

**HARVEST HOUSE PUBLISHERS**
Eugene, Oregon 97402

All biblical quotations from the Holy Bible: New International Version.
Copyright 1978 by the New York International Bible Society.
Used by permission of Zondervan Bible Publishers.

Cover photo by David Muench

# Foreword

Even though mankind has been making progress in technology, transportation, communication, and medical science, I sometimes wonder how long this old world of ours will keep going on. Hundreds of thousands still die of starvation every year. Diseases take a huge toll of human life. Children suffer. Man's inhumanity to man is still evident in even the most advanced nations. Wars abound. Most people are living with the vague feeling that some major change is about to take place.

According to the Bible, a new day is coming! The rapture of the church is next on God's prophetic timetable. Then will follow the tribulation, the judgment of the nations, the restoration of Israel, the glorious return of Christ, and the millennial kingdom.

The survey of endtime events found in this book will acquaint you with the biblical teaching about that coming new day. I recommend it highly, and I encourage you to read it carefully. How thankful we can be for the blessed hope of Christ's return, which will usher in that wonderful new day!

Richard W. De Haan

# Contents

# Preface

Where is human history going? Is man traveling down the road to a catastrophic end? Or are we headed for a golden age of worldwide peace, universal prosperity, and perfect righteousness?

Most thinking people today answer these questions pessimistically. They believe that man will bring about his own destruction through a nuclear holocaust or by environmental pollution. Even among Christians, many take a dim view of earth's future. Although they don't foresee the total annihilation of the race, they do expect that major disasters will continue until Christ returns.

Some believers, however, are convinced that this earth will one day enjoy a wonderful era totally free from desolating wars, frightful diseases, and cruel injustices. I am one of this company. I believe the day is coming when Jesus Christ will return to this earth as King of kings and Lord of lords, take the reins of government, and usher in 1,000 years of universal blessedness. Because God created the earth and man for His glory, the millennial age will be a suitable close for this phase of human history. It will also be the vestibule into the absolute and eternal perfection of the new heavens and new earth, which are portrayed in Revelation 21 and 22 as replacing our present planetary system. Yes, *there's a new day coming!*

# 1. The Rapture of the Church

I am convinced that the next event on God's endtime calendar is the rapture of the church—the "catching up" of all believers for a glorious meeting with Christ in the air. I believe this event is imminent; that is, it could take place at any moment. The rapture will be followed by a brief period of history marked by the rule of a cruel world dictator, by fierce persecution of people who turn in faith to the Lord Jesus, and by devastating supernatural judgments. This time of tribulation will be concluded by the glorious return of Christ to destroy the wicked and to establish His 1,000-year reign over the earth.

There was a time when I didn't think in terms of two distinct comings of Christ separated by a period of great tribulation. Nor did I anticipate a golden age of universal peace, prosperity, and righteousness under His rule. I viewed the return of Jesus Christ as the grand finale of human history on our planet. I believed that the Lord, acting in rapid sequence, would raise the believing dead of all the ages, translate living Christians, kill the unbelievers still living on the earth, resurrect the unsaved, judge all mankind to determine each individual's eternal destiny, burn up our present earth-system with fire, bring in the new heavens and new earth, welcome the redeemed to their eternal home, and cast the unsaved into the lake of fire. I knew that some people believed the Lord's return would take place in two stages and involve an earthly millennial reign of Christ, but I assumed they were wrong.

When I was still a teenager, however, a friend said something about Christ's second coming that may have been a factor in leading me to my present position. It happened on a warm Sunday evening after our church service. Four of us were walking down Grandville Avenue in Grand Rapids discussing the usual subjects: cars, girls, current issues, and religion. I don't recall the exact context, but I do remember that Lewis, our intellectual leader, addressed the three of us with this question: "Do you believe Jesus may come back tonight?" My reply came without hesitation, "No! He can't come till the end of the great tribulation of Matthew 24." The other two fellows agreed that we weren't in the great tribulation, and that this had to precede Christ's return. Lewis then said, "Well, it's unanimous. We're all convinced that the Lord won't return tonight. And Jesus said He would come back in a moment when 'ye think not.'"

I remembered reading this verse (Matthew 24:44), and I began to do some serious thinking. How could the Lord's return catch people by surprise if it were to be preceded by the most terrible time of tribulation the world has ever seen, including the supernatural signs given in Matthew 24? It seemed to me that if I were to hear in the news that a man who matched the biblical description of Antichrist had gained enough power to be a world dictator, I would start looking up. Then, if I saw strange sights in the heavens, devastating acts of divine judgment, and a dreadful persecution of all who wouldn't worship an image set up by this world ruler, I'd surely get ready for Christ's return. With all this evidence, I would never be caught by surprise.

I began to see that Christ's statements about His

coming without warning didn't jibe with my understanding of His distinct predictions of the great tribulation and the rise of Antichrist as signs of its nearness.
Little by little, I came to believe that there was only
one way I could harmonize the passages which speak of
the unexpectedness of the Lord's return with the verses
that say awesome events will immediately precede it. I
had to distinguish clearly between the Lord's coming
for His own and His return in glory to rule over the
earth.

In this chapter, I will discuss the first stage in the
second coming of Christ. We usually refer to it as the
rapture, a term that expresses the idea of a "catching
up." I will set forth four characteristics of the rapture
that are distinct from Christ's return in glory.

## A SELECTIVE EVENT

First, the rapture will be characterized by selectivity.
Only believers will experience resurrection and translation when the trumpet sounds. Jesus gave this very
special promise to His disciples: "And if I go and prepare a place for you, I will come back and take you to be
with Me that you also may be where I am" (John 14:3).
Paul spoke of this event in 1 Thessalonians 4:13-18 and
1 Corinthians 15:51-54. Note especially these en-
couraging words: ". . . the dead in Christ will rise first.
After that, we who are still alive and are left will be
caught up with them in the clouds to meet the Lord in
the air" (1 Thessalonians 4:16,17). "We will not all
sleep, but we will all be changed—in a flash, in the
twinkling of an eye, at the last trumpet. For the trumpet will sound, the dead will be raised imperishable,
and we will be changed" (1 Corinthians 15:51,52). Not
one word appears in these passages about the resurrection or the judgment of the unsaved. How different
from Revelation 20:11-15! Here the apostle John portrayed the great white throne judgment, the final
resurrection, and the eternal destiny of the unsaved.
The rapture will be selective, however, taking only believers in Christ.

Now, this "catching up" of Christians from among mankind is sometimes referred to as a "secret rapture" by both friend and foe of this viewpoint. I see this as unfortunate and inaccurate. The rapture will not be secret in any sense of the term. This coming of Jesus for His own will be accompanied by "a loud command," "the voice of the archangel," and "the trumpet call of God" (1 Thessalonians 4:16).

Some Bible students say that only Christians will hear this call of command and trumpet sound. They may be right, but we can't be sure. Furthermore, even if non-Christians don't hear these sounds, they will be made vividly aware of a tremendous occurrence. Many people will suddenly disappear. In those parts of the world where the rapture takes place during the night, the disruption will be less evident than where it is daytime. In all walks of life, believers will be missed. Cars will be left without drivers, planes without pilots, machines without operators, and classrooms without teachers. Perhaps the ground above the graves where the bodies of Christians have been interred will be opened, not to release the new body but to show the unsaved what happened. It may even be possible that pieces of clothing will be left behind as mute evidence, just as the graveclothes in the sepulcher gave testimony to our Lord's resurrection. In any case, the rapture will be selective, but not secret.

## AN IMMINENT EVENT

The second characteristic of the rapture is its imminency. This means that it is an any-moment possibility. The motto, "Perhaps Today" is correct. Believers in every generation of church history have looked for the return of Christ for His own.

Some people who do not accept the doctrine of imminency argue that believers in the early church could not have hoped for Christ's sudden return. They point out that passages like Psalm 2 portray an age that separated Christ's resurrection from His return—a period of time when Messiah would sit with the

Father on the throne in heaven. They also refer to our Lord's warnings to His disciples that they would experience a time of tribulation and persecution. Jesus even told Peter that he would be executed when he became old (John 21:18). All of these predictions required time for their fulfillment. Therefore, the doubters claim these first Christians could not have been expecting an any-moment return of Christ.

These objections to the doctrine of imminency are valid only when applied to the first few years of church history. But this was just a brief period! By the time Paul began writing his epistles, he considered the return of the Lord Jesus to be truly imminent. The risen Lord had been seated at the Father's right hand for several years. The gospel had been proclaimed throughout the Roman world. Paul and the other apostles had suffered for the sake of Christ. Peter had reached the age where he could be termed "old" in a time when the lifespan was much shorter than it is now. (Paul in his letter to Philemon spoke of himself as "an old man" though he was perhaps only in his fifties.)

True, Peter had not yet been executed in fulfillment of Jesus' prediction. But how many people at any given time would have known this? They were living in a time of persecution. Many Christians were being imprisoned and put to death. The only ones who could have known that Peter was still alive were the few who lived in close contact with him. From A.D. 50 onward, therefore, the Lord's prophecy about Peter's execution could not have been a hindrance to belief in imminency.

The doctrine of imminency was taught by the Lord Jesus. He repeatedly instructed His followers to be ready always for His return, underscoring this point through parables and illustrations. He compared His disciples to servants waiting for the any-moment return of their master from a wedding banquet (Luke 12:35-38). He emphasized the need for readiness by telling of a homeowner who was robbed because he had not taken proper precautions against a break-in (Luke 12:39,40). He contrasted two servants—one who lived in daily expectation of his master's return and the other who grew careless (Luke 12:42-48). In each case, the return was sudden and unexpected. In each case, the person who was ready was given rewards while the one who wasn't ready was punished. Yes, Jesus certainly taught the doctrine of imminency.

By warning His disciples to be ready at all times, and by giving them the signs of His return in glory, our Lord let it be known that His second coming would take place in two stages. True, He never stated this truth in so many words. But this was for a good reason: it was not yet time for God to reveal the full truth about the church. Therefore, Jesus expressed prophetic truth in the manner of the Old Testament prophets. He brought separate events together into one picture without distinguishing them. For example, the prophets often spoke of the suffering and death of Christ and of His return in glory, without giving a hint that they would be separated by centuries. They also depicted a near-at-hand occurrence and another many centuries later without indicating their chronological placement. An example of this appeared in Isaiah 7.

*Therefore the Lord Himself will give you a sign: The virgin will be with child and will give birth to a son, and will call Him Immanuel. He will eat curds and honey when He knows enough to reject the wrong and choose the right. But before the boy knows enough to reject the wrong and choose the right, the land of the two kings you dread will be laid waste (Isaiah 7:14-16).*

The prophet spoke of a virgin-born Son who will be called Immanuel, and of a boy who would eat "curds and honey" when he was old enough "to reject the wrong and choose the right." Orthodox Bible scholars are all agreed that the virgin-born Son called Immanuel is none other than Jesus Christ, as stated in Matthew 1:23. Furthermore, they agree that the boy who would eat curds and honey when still a young man was a son of Isaiah named Maher-shalal-hash-baz (Isaiah 8). When enemy invaders swept through a land, they took the grain and most of the sheep along with their prisoners. The people left behind had only curds (a product made from the milk of the goats that had not been taken) and wild honey to eat. And before Isaiah's son was old enough to choose between right and wrong, Assyria had desolated both Samaria and Syria.

More than 500 years separated the fulfillments of the prophecies about Maher-shalal-hash-baz and Jesus Christ. Yet Isaiah portrayed them in one picture with no clear indication of their time relationship. Prophecy was not intended to be pre-written history. The prophets themselves often didn't understand exactly how the events they portrayed would be related to one another. And until they become clear in their fulfillment, neither can we.

Jesus was using the methodology of the Old Testament prophets when He brought the two stages of His return together into one picture. In God's program, the time had not yet arrived for the revelation of the full truth about the church as an entity distinct from Israel. Jesus therefore presented the truth about the rapture and the return without saying anything about their time relationship.

Before leaving the subject of imminency, let's think about this doctrine as it relates to the "signs of the times." Some Bible students today are preoccupied with these signs. They boldly declare their belief, on the basis of current world conditions, that the Lord's return is very near at hand. They are sure that the great tribulation depicted in Matthew 24 must be right around the corner. Some of those who think the church will go through this terrible time are even urging believers to get ready for a nuclear war and famine by building bomb shelters, stockpiling large quantities of food, and arming themselves to shoot desperate neighbors who may wish to share their place of refuge or provisions.

The Bible students who believe in a pre-tribulation rapture but are always looking at the "signs of the times" can build an impressive case for their contention that the age will end very soon. Israel is a nation in

Palestine. Russia, depicted in Ezekiel 38 and 39 as mounting an attack against Israel and being supernaturally defeated, has become a world power. A group of countries in Western Europe are allied in a common market, forming the basis for what could easily be the nucleus of Antichrist's empire. Technology is making the nations so interdependent that a centralized world government seems inevitable. Then too, moral and spiritual conditions throughout the world match those that the Scriptures depict as prevailing at the close of our dispensation.

What about these "signs of the times"? Let me begin by saying that they certainly do give us good reason for believing that the return of our Savior may be very near. The world stage does appear to be set for the fulfillment of Scripture's great endtime prophecies. But we must be careful about making predictions.

Many have done so throughout the course of church history and have been embarrassed when their predictions were wrong. In addition, these signs cannot become the basis for our belief in imminency. The Lord could come for His own at any moment—even if Russia were reduced to a second-rate power, Israel were pushed out of Palestine, a great revival of Christianity occurred, and the moral climate throughout the world changed for the better. This is because the "signs of the times," the prophecies of famine, earthquakes, celestial disturbances, fierce persecution, and moral degeneration refer primarily to the great tribulation, which I believe will follow the rapture of the church. Therefore, even though these "signs" give us reason to believe the Lord's coming may be very near, they are not the basis for our belief in imminency.

I am dismayed by the way some Bible teachers use "signs of the times" to make specific predictions relating to our Lord's return. A few years ago some of them put together Israel's birth as a nation in 1948 with these words of Jesus:

*Now learn this lesson from the fig tree: As soon as its twigs get tender and its leaves come out, you know that*

*summer is near. Even so, when you see all these things,*
*you know that it is near, right at the door. I tell you the*
*truth, this generation will certainly not pass away until*
*all these things have happened (Matthew 24:32-34).*

These Bible scholars made the fig tree represent Israel
and its budding her emergence as a nation in 1948.
They then interpreted our Lord's words, "... this generation will certainly not pass away until all these things
have happened," as meaning that all our Lord's prophecies would be fulfilled within a timespan of about 40
years from 1948. Since they view the tribulation as a
7-year period, they came dangerously close to setting a
date for the rapture—somewhere around 1981. But
their conclusions were unwarranted. They were based
upon an erroneous interpretation of Christ's words.
And the Bible students who propounded this view may
cause many people to doubt the truthfulness of the
Bible and the integrity of God's servants.

Yes, the signs of the times *may* seem to be indicating
the soon return of Jesus Christ. But then again, they
may not. Many of God's children are praying for a great
revival of the church. If the Lord answers these
prayers, we will see multitudes converted to Christ and
a change in the moral climate throughout the world.
Besides, God may prevent the outbreak of a nuclear
war in our generation. And He may open new doors for
the preaching of the gospel. Therefore, my conviction is
that we should believe and teach *imminency,* not
*immediacy.* We should be ready for the rapture, but we
should also pray and work and plan with future generations in mind.

## A WELCOME DELIVERANCE

We have seen that the rapture will be selective and
that it is imminent. The Bible teaches that it will also
be a welcome deliverance. It will take the Lord's people
from the earth before His wrath is poured out upon it.
This assurance is expressed in 1 Thessalonians 5.

*Now, brothers, about times and dates we do not need to*
*write to you, for you know very well that the day of the*

*Lord will come like a thief in the night. While people are saying, "Peace and safety," destruction will come on them suddenly, as labor pains on a pregnant woman, and they will not escape.*

*But you, brothers, are not in darkness so that this day should surprise you like a thief. You are all sons of the light and sons of the day. We do not belong to the night or to the darkness. So then, let us not be like others, who are asleep, but let us be alert and self-controlled. For those who sleep, sleep at night, and those who get drunk, get drunk at night. But since we belong to the day, let us be self-controlled, putting on faith and love as a breastplate, and the hope of salvation as a helmet. For God did not appoint us to suffer wrath but to receive salvation through our Lord Jesus Christ. He died for us so that, whether we are awake or asleep, we may live together with Him (1 Thessalonians 5:1-10).*

Most Bible scholars interpret the phrase "God did not appoint us to suffer wrath but to receive salvation through our Lord Jesus Christ" as a declaration that we have not been destined to the wrath of hell. I believe, however, that this passage relates more directly to the wrath of the tribulation period. I take this view on the basis of the context of this sentence, which is about the Lord's return.

We have already discussed 1 Thessalonians 4:13-18, where the apostle assured the Christians in Thessalonica that those who died in Christ will share fully in the blessedness of His return for His own. Paul further reminded his readers that they had been given enough information about the second coming to look forward to it with joy rather than fear. Although the day of the Lord will come upon unbelievers as a thief in the night and plunge them into deep distress, it will be a blessed occasion for Christians.

The term "day of the Lord" has a wide range of meaning in the Old Testament. It denotes a time of Divine intervention, both in blessing for believers and in judgment upon the unredeemed. In Joel 2, for example, the day of the Lord is a time of "darkness and gloom" (v. 2) for the unsaved and a time of deliverance and salvation for the redeemed (vv. 21-27). The term "day of the Lord" depicts both the great tribulation and the millennium. With this in mind, we can understand why Paul in 1 Thessalonians 5 portrayed the day of the Lord as that terrible time of God's wrath upon the unsaved while also picturing it as a marvelous deliverance for Christians.

The promise of 1 Thessalonians 5:9, "God did not appoint us to suffer wrath but to receive salvation," relates to the great tribulation, not to eternal damnation. Believers are not destined to taste God's wrath—neither in the great tribulation nor in hell. Christ paid the full price for our sins. God may chasten us, but He will never punish us or make us the objects of His wrath. The judgments of the "day of the Lord" are indeed expressions of God's wrath. In Zephaniah 1:15 we read, "That day will be a day of wrath, a day of distress and anguish, a day of trouble and ruin, a day of darkness and gloom, a day of clouds and blackness." Since God has not appointed us to wrath, we can look for the rapture to deliver us from it.

## A NECESSARY REMOVAL

Fourth, the rapture may be characterized as a necessary removal. Before Antichrist can be revealed and the judgments of the day of the Lord be poured out, the Holy Spirit—as He indwells the church—must be removed from the earth. Paul gave us this information in 2 Thessalonians 2.

*Concerning the coming of our Lord Jesus Christ and our being gathered to Him, we ask you, brothers, not to become easily unsettled or alarmed by some prophecy, report or letter supposed to have come from us, saying that the day of the Lord has already come. Don't let anyone deceive you in any way, for that day will not come until the rebellion occurs and the man of lawlessness is revealed, the man doomed to destruction. He opposes and exalts himself over everything that is called God or is worshiped, and even sets himself up in God's temple, proclaiming himself to be God.*

*Don't you remember that when I was with you I used to tell you these things? And now you know what is holding him back, so that he may be revealed at the proper time. For the secret power of lawlessness is already at work; but the One who now holds it back will continue to do so till He is taken out of the way. And then the lawless one will be revealed, whom the Lord Jesus will overthrow with the breath of His mouth and destroy by the splendor of His coming (2 Thessalonians 2:1-8).*

Paul included this paragraph in his letter because he had heard that some Christians in Thessalonica were afraid they had entered the judgment time of the day of the Lord. They were undergoing persecution, and they were getting reports that confused them. They were being told that the persecution was an indication that they had entered the terrible time of judgment foretold by the Old Testament prophets. But in Paul's first letter to the Thessalonians he had told them that the rapture would occur before this awesome period, delivering them from it. No wonder they were asking questions!

The apostle assured the Thessalonian Christians that their fears were groundless. He reminded them that the great tribulation could not come until "the rebellion occurs and the man of lawlessness is revealed." Passages like Daniel 9 and 11, Matthew 24, and Revelation 13 tell us that Antichrist will set up an image representing himself, demand that it be worshiped, and initiate a program of terrible persecution against all who refuse. This open declaration of war on those who will believe on Jesus Christ begins the period we call "the great tribulation."

Before the rebellion and revealing of Antichrist takes place, however, the Restrainer must be taken "out of the way." The "mystery of iniquity," the lawless system which will culminate in Antichrist, has been in operation for thousands of years. But the forces of evil, which are being held in check by the Restrainer, will be unleashed in all their fury when He is taken "out of the way." The Restrainer is the Holy Spirit, who indwells believers and makes them the salt of the earth.

Many Bible students are unwilling to come to this conclusion, so they have advanced other ideas as to the identity of the source of restraint. Some have suggested that Paul was referring to the Roman Empire. But Antichrist was not revealed when Rome fell. Others have declared that the Restrainer is human government, but human government will continue after Antichrist is revealed. The Restrainer certainly cannot be Satan. The only plausible explanation is that the Restrainer is the Holy Spirit as He holds back the forces of iniquity through His indwelling presence in believers. When the church is taken up from the earth in the rapture, the restraint the Holy Spirit exercises through it will be removed. Even so, the Spirit, who is the third person of the trinity, will continue to empower the Word of God as it is proclaimed. He will still work in the regeneration and sanctification of those who put their trust in Christ. He will enable them to stand true in spite of dreadful persecution. Only His restraining influence through the believers who make up the church will be removed.

The New International Version of the Bible is correct in translating the Greek phrase *he apostasia* in 2 Thessalonians 2:3 as "the rebellion." Some Bible scholars have rendered it "the departure," making it a reference to the rapture. They paraphrase Paul's statement as follows: "The day of the Lord can't come until the rapture occurs and the man of sin is revealed." While I agree with the sentiment, I don't believe that this is a proper translation. I wish it were, because it would convince everybody that the rapture will indeed precede the great tribulation. But a careful and honest study of the word *apostasia* has led me to conclude that it connotes only a certain kind of departure—one with negative overtones. In Acts 21:21, the other place this phrase occurs in the New Testament, it describes the charge made against Paul that he was teaching "all the Jews who live among the Gentiles *to turn away* from Moses." It is a departure in the sense of a turning away from, a rejection, or a rebellion.

In summary, we have defined the rapture as the "catching up" of church saints—both those who have died and those who are still living on the earth. Believers who have "fallen asleep" in Jesus will receive their resurrection bodies an instant before living believers are transformed. They will rise together to meet the Lord in the air.

The rapture can easily be distinguished from the Lord's return in glory. We have seen that it is an imminent event, a selective occurrence, a welcome deliverance, and a necessary removal. This means that it could take place at any moment, that it will involve only believers, that it will deliver the Lord's people from the wrath of the great tribulation, and that it will make possible the revealing of Antichrist by the removing of the Restrainer. The rapture is our blessed hope. Let's live in continual readiness so that "when He appears we may be confident and unashamed before Him at His coming" (1 John 2:28).

# 2. The Revealing of Antichrist

I recently received a pamphlet through the mail in which the author boldly declared that "the Christ" is now living on our planet, and that he is "about to reveal himself." The author described this "Christ" as a modern man who represents all religions. He claimed that he is the composite of the man called Jesus Christ by Christians, "Krishna" by Hindus, "the Messiah" by Jews, "Imam Mahdi" by the Moslems, and "the Fifth Buddha" by Buddhists. Followers of this contemporary "Christ" say that after living for ages as a celestial being in a "body of light," he took upon himself a "body of manifestation," descended, and spent some time in the Himalayas. He now supposedly dwells in the Indo-Pakistani section of London, and he is said to be preparing to make himself known.

This claim is preposterous! Jesus of Nazareth is the only true Christ, and He declared unequivocally that His return to this planet will not take place secretly. When He comes to rapture the church, He will come with "a loud command, with the voice of the archangel and with the trumpet call of God" (1 Thessalonians 4:16). Besides, the people who are unsaved will be

21

amazed at the sudden disappearance of many thousands of Christians. A few years later, when our Lord returns to take over the reins of government, He will do so in a manner so public that "every eye will see Him, even those who pierced Him; and all the peoples of the earth will mourn because of Him" (Revelation 1:7).

Our Lord anticipated wild claims like the one I mentioned above. He said, "Watch out that no one deceives you. For many will come in My name claiming, 'I am the Christ,' and will deceive many. So if anyone tells you, 'There he is, out in the desert,' do not go out; or, 'Here he is, in the inner rooms,' do not believe it. For as the lightning comes from the east, and flashes to the west, so will be the coming of the Son of Man. Wherever there is a carcass, there the vultures will gather" (Matthew 24:4,5,26-28).

All secret "messiahs" are impostors. Many such men have appeared through the course of church history, and the apostle John labeled them as antichrists when he wrote, "Dear children, this is the last hour; and as you have heard that the Antichrist is coming, even now many antichrists have come" (1 John 2:18). These men are forerunners of the one man who will be *the* Antichrist. We do not know where this Antichrist will rise to power, nor have we been told the date when he will make his appearance. The man in London to whom I referred is simply raising one more false alarm—he is an antichrist. But one day the real Antichrist of biblical prophecy will be revealed.

In this chapter we will discover what kind of man this coming Antichrist will be by examining the Bible passages that speak of him. We won't find any information about his physical characteristics, whether he will be short or tall, dark-skinned or white, bald or curly-topped. But we will get a fairly accurate picture of him by considering his personality traits. Remember, the Bible tells us that he will receive his power and throne and authority from Satan, and he will lead mankind to worship both the devil and himself (see Revelation 13:2,4). Because he is Satan's man, we can expect to see a sharp contrast between him and our Lord. This wicked man will be characterized by aggressiveness, blasphemy, superstition, cruelty, and self-will—traits that make him the absolute antithesis to Jesus Christ. Let's look at these five traits more carefully.

## AGGRESSIVENESS

As Antichrist rises to a place of international power, he will demonstrate that he is aggressive and resourceful. In Revelation 6:2 he is portrayed as riding on a white horse, holding a bow, wearing a crown, and riding out "as a conqueror bent on conquest." He will be so impressive and successful that a large segment of mankind will actually worship him. As the devil's personal envoy, he will be an expert in human manipulation—so much so that mankind in general will kneel before him, saying, "Who is like the beast? Who can make war against him?" (Revelation 13:4).

Antichrist will be the kind of self-confident leader that people turn to in times of crisis. Humans are always impressed by capable and aggressive men. They like strong rulers such as Alexander the Great, Caesar, Napoleon, Hitler, Mussolini, and Stalin. What a contrast between this coming Antichrist and the Lord Jesus! Our Savior didn't enter the earthly scene in pomp or splendor. He came into our world in a stable, grew up in a poor home in Nazareth, worked in a carpenter shop until He was 30 years old, and began His public ministry with 12 common men as His apostles. He dressed in peasant garb. He didn't make it easy for people to follow Him. When He rode into Jerusalem amid the enthusiastic shouts of His followers, He sat on a lowly donkey instead of a magnificent white horse. He permitted men to mock Him, scourge Him, and crucify Him on a Roman cross. In so doing, He was true to the description given Him by the Old Testament prophet Isaiah and quoted in Matthew 12:19,20. "He will not quarrel or cry out; no one will hear His voice in the streets. A bruised reed He will not break, and a smoldering wick He will not snuff out, till He leads justice to victory." He set the pattern for us, and we are to follow His example as we apply the Beatitudes He gave. They promise blessing to the "poor in spirit," "those who mourn," and to the "meek" (Matthew 5:3-5). In sharp contrast, Antichrist will follow the evil pattern of the cruel world dictators of the past.

I believe the world stage has been set for the appearance of an aggressive, strong, dynamic leader. People in general are afraid of nuclear war and worsening economic conditions. They are fearful as they observe the startling technological advances in weaponry. They are afraid to die because they have departed from the Judeo-Christian view of life. They are beginning to realize that the nations are becoming increasingly interdependent in economics. One of these days, therefore, they will welcome a powerful man who can apparently bring them peace and prosperity. As an aggressive leader, Antichrist will appear to be the hope of the world. Then, when he has firmly established his position, and has forged his way to the top he will show his true colors. As we have already seen, this will not happen until the church has been raptured.

## BLASPHEMY

Antichrist will also be a man of gross blasphemy. As soon as he feels secure in his position of leadership, he will boldly and arrogantly express his disdain for God. He will also initiate programs that will make it clear to all that he hates God and His people. The Bible gives us some specific attitudes of Antichrist that demonstrate his blasphemous nature. We will look briefly at several of them.

### Contempt for God's Prophetic Program

One way Antichrist will express his hatred of God will be to show his contempt for the prophetic program outlined in the Scriptures. Even though he knows full well that the Lord has a special role for Israel in the kingdom age, he will try to frustrate that program by annihilating the Jewish people. Because he will need the support of the Jews as he rises to world power, however,

he will make a 7-year treaty with Israel. He may even
do so with the full knowledge that this event is predicted in Daniel 9:27. Blinded by Satan, he may be deluded
into thinking that he can overcome God by sticking to a
carefully thought-out plan of conciliation. He will let
the Jews build a temple in Jerusalem. He will allow
them to institute a system of sacrifices and offerings.
He will gain their trust. But suddenly he will turn
against them. He will force them to stop their sacrifices
and offerings. He will taunt and humiliate them by
placing an image in their temple and demanding that
they worship it. We read:

> *He will confirm a covenant with many for one "seven,"*
> *but in the middle of that "seven" he will put an end to*
> *sacrifice and offering. And one who causes desolation*
> *will place abominations on a wing of the temple until*
> *the end that is decreed is poured out on him*
> *(Daniel 9:27).*

Although this verse doesn't tell us specifically that Antichrist will set up an idol in the Jewish temple, it
refers to this event in the words, "And one who causes
desolation will place abominations on a wing of the
temple." Jesus pointed out that the image will be
placed in their restored temple when He said, "So when
you see standing in the holy place 'the abomination
that causes desolation,' spoken of through the prophet
Daniel—let the reader understand—then let those who
are in Judea flee to the mountains" (Matthew
24:15,16). This bold act of Antichrist will set off the
great tribulation. He will dare to commit this terrible
act of blasphemy because he will be convinced that he
has the power to thwart God.

## Disdain for all Religions of History

The second element in the blasphemous conduct of Antichrist will be his arrogant disdain for all the religions
of history. Translated quite literally from the Hebrew,
Daniel 11:37 reads, "And for the gods of his fathers he
shall have no regard; nor for the desire of women; nor
for any god at all shall he have regard. For he shall

exalt himself above everything." The noted commentator Leupold says, "In this verse the unnaturalness of this ruler is now presented." He points out that most people show a measure of respect for religion, especially the faiths that have stood through thousands of years. This man, however, will boldly reject every historical religious system. Daniel, in fact, made the sweeping statement, ". . . nor will he regard any god, but will exalt himself above them all." What bold blasphemy!

*A Perverted Lifestyle*

I believe Antichrist will further blaspheme God by adopting a wicked, perverted lifestyle. In the middle of this verse (which tells of Antichrist's attitude toward believing in God as expressed throughout history) is the declaration that he will have no regard "for the desire of women" (literal rendering of the Hebrew text). The NIV translation, "the one desired by women," implies that Antichrist will show no respect for the god Tammu, or Adonis, who was especially worshiped by women in ancient days. This may be a correct interpretation, but it isn't a literal translation. I have serious doubts about this rendering because we have no evidence that people will go back to worshiping the pantheon of Babylonian and Greek gods.

If we are to take this expression literally, we must try to determine what "desire of women" Antichrist rejects. Some of the commentators of past centuries said that he would show contempt for the women's natural desire for marriage and children by forbidding marriage. A number of today's scholars believe he will show no regard for human affection and tenderness, virtues highly prized by women. However, I personally believe he will express his disdain for "the desire of women" to marry and have children by advocating and living the homosexual lifestyle. The fact that this statement about his showing no regard for "the desire of women" occurs in such a close relationship to his blasphemous activities makes me think in terms of an open promotion of homosexuality. What more could a person do to show his blatant disrespect for God?

*The Abomination of Desolation*

Antichrist will also blaspheme God by placing an idol in the restored Jewish temple and demanding that people worship it. This is the specific act that is referred to in the Bible as the "abomination of desolation." As we saw earlier, Jesus referred to it in His Olivet discourse (Matthew 24:15,16). And Paul declared of Antichrist that he "opposes and exalts himself over everything that is called God or is worshiped, and even sets himself up in God's temple, proclaiming himself to be God" (2 Thessalonians 2:4). Further in Revelation 13:5 we read, "The beast was given a mouth to utter proud words and blasphemies and to exercise his authority for forty-two months. He opened his mouth to blaspheme God, and to slander His name and His dwelling place and those who live in heaven" (Revelation 13:5,6). The apex of his blasphemy will be the erection of this idol in the holy place of the temple that will be built in Jerusalem.

Antichrist will be the the most brazen blasphemer of all history. The passion of his life will be his desire to insult the Almighty by word and deed. In sharp contrast, the Lord Jesus showed the utmost respect and reverence for the Father. Bringing glory to Him was the passion of His life.

## SUPERSTITION

In spite of all his bold public blasphemies, Antichrist will likely be a superstitious and fear-filled man. The Scriptures seem to indicate that even though he is outwardly God-denying and atheistic, he will privately engage in some kind of worship. Daniel wrote:

> *The king will do as he pleases.... He will show no regard for the gods of his fathers or for the one desired by women, nor will he regard any god, but will exalt himself above them all. Instead of them, he will honor a god of fortresses; a god unknown to his fathers he will honor with gold and silver, with precious stones and costly gifts. He will attack the mightiest fortresses with the help of a foreign god and will greatly honor those*

*who acknowledge him. He will make them rulers over*
*many people and will distribute the land at a price*
*(Daniel 11:36-39).*

Although Antichrist will declare himself to be God, he
will nevertheless honor "a god of fortresses," bringing
to it gold, silver, precious stones, and costly gifts. With
the "help" of this foreign god, he makes conquest after
conquest. But just who or what is this "god of
fortresses"? Some say that it is his war machine. They
contend that he will honor his military power by
pouring vast funds into it and trusting it to help him
achieve his goals. But the idea of worshiping armies
and munitions seems a bit incongruous. Furthermore,
we are told that it is "with the help of a foreign god"
that he gains his territory. How could his own war
machine be called "a foreign god"?

My personal belief is that Antichrist will worship
some kind of deity in secret. This passage depicts the
contrast between what he is in public and what he is in
private. Outwardly, he will be a bold atheist; secretly,
he will be a fearful and superstitious follower of the
occult. As Satan's right-hand man, he will undoubtedly
worship him. This will get him into a wide range of
practices associated with Satanism. In this respect he
will be similar to Adolf Hitler. This Nazi leader never
openly acknowledged any dependence upon the
supernatural, but he secretly consulted fortune tellers,
dabbled in the occult, and made major decisions
involving many thousands of lives on the basis of
astrological readings.

## CRUELTY

The third characteristic of Antichrist will be his
fiendish cruelty. Revelation 13 presents this terrible
picture of him with remarkable clarity. It begins with
the description of his awesome power to make war on
the saints. We read:

*He was given power to make war against the saints and*
*to conquer them. And he was given authority over every*
*tribe, people, language and nation. All inhabitants of*

*the earth will worship the beast—all whose names have not been written in the book of life belonging to the Lamb that was slain from the creation of the world.*

*He who has an ear, let him hear.*

*If anyone is to go into captivity, into captivity he will go. If anyone is to be killed with the sword, with the sword he will be killed.*

*This calls for patient endurance and faithfulness on the part of the saints (Revelation 13:7-10).*

Although Antichrist will apparently receive the worship of the majority of the people, he will still find great numbers who refuse to bow down to him. This will arouse his wrath, leading him to do his utmost to find and kill every one of them.

This same chapter also shows his cruelty through the agency of the "second beast," the man called the false prophet in Revelation 19:20 and 20:10. From Revelation 13 we read:

*He ordered them [the inhabitants of the earth] to set up an image in honor of the beast who was wounded by the sword and yet lived. He was given power to give breath to the image of the first beast, so that it could speak and cause all who refused to worship the image to be killed. He also forced everyone, small and great, rich and poor, free and slave, to receive a mark on his right hand or on his forehead, so that no one could buy or sell unless he had the mark, which is the name of the beast or the number of his name.*

*This calls for wisdom. If anyone has insight, let him calculate the number of the beast, for it is man's number. His number is 666 (Revelation 13:14-18).*

The false prophet will not only demand that people worship the image of the beast, he will also set up an identification system designed to flush out for execution all who refuse to give him homage.

With ruthless abandon, Antichrist, aided and abetted by the false prophet, will succeed in killing hundreds of thousands of people. The martyrs portrayed in Revelation 6:9-11 and the white-robed multitude presented in Revelation 7:9-17 are the people he will kill.

John identified this martyred number as those "who have come out of the great tribulation" (7:14).

Antichrist will be barbaric in his cruelty toward God's people. But the Lord will protect a remnant of His own from among both Jews and Gentiles. He will keep them safe so they can become the citizens of the earthly kingdom that Christ will establish at His glorious return.

## SELF-WILLED

A final characteristic of Antichrist is his willfulness. He will want his way, and he will go to any length necessary to achieve it. This extreme determination to have his way is closely related to his aggressiveness, which we have already discussed. Antichrist will always seek to do his own will. (By contrast, Jesus Christ always sought to do His Father's will.) This self-centeredness will certainly be a factor in helping Antichrist attain his position, but it will also bring about his doom. He is the man presented in Daniel 11:36 as the "willful king." He will achieve a degree of success even though he blasphemes God and fights Him, but he will soon meet his Waterloo. We read:

> At the time of the end the king of the South will engage him in battle, and the king of the North will storm out against him with chariots and cavalry and a great fleet of ships. He will invade many countries and sweep through them like a flood. He will also invade the Beautiful Land. Many countries will fall, but Edom, Moab and the leaders of Ammon will be delivered from his hand. He will extend his power over many countries; Egypt will not escape. He will gain control of the treasures of gold and silver and all the riches of Egypt, with the Libyans and Nubians in submission. But reports from the east and the north will alarm him, and he will set out in a great rage to destroy and annihilate many. He will pitch his royal tents between the seas at the beautiful holy mountain. Yet he will come to his end, and no one will help him
> (Daniel 11:40-45).

In his determination to maintain complete supremacy, Antichrist will act quickly and decisively to quell all opposition. But from the book of Revelation we learn that while he is keeping his position secure, he is being hurt by the terrible divine judgments falling on the earth. It should be obvious to Antichrist that the Lord will be victorious. But he will be so consumed by his determination to oppose God and His people that he will keep fighting until he meets his doom at Armageddon. There he and his armies will be destroyed by the returning Lord Jesus and His hosts from heaven. They will cast him and the false prophet into the lake of fire. A mighty angel will bind the devil and throw him into the abyss, where he will remain for a thousand years.

To summarize, Antichrist will be the absolute antithesis to Jesus Christ. He will be aggressive, blasphemous, superstitious, cruel, and self-willed. Of all humans, he will be the consummate enemy of God. He is the second person in the evil triad along with the devil and the false prophet. He will be sent into the world by Satan, just as the Lord Jesus was sent into the world by the Father (John 6:57). He will receive from Satan "his power and his throne," just as the Son received from the Father "all authority in heaven and in earth" (Matthew 28:18-20). He will be magnified by the false prophet, just as the Son is glorified by the Holy Spirit (John 16:14).

Yes, Antichrist will indeed be Satan's counterpart to Jesus Christ. He will achieve a remarkable degree of success toward his evil purposes for a brief period of time. But his end will come quickly, and his cohorts will share his fate. Antichrist will lead his followers to eternal death; the Lord Jesus will lead all who place their trust in Him into everlasting life. What an amazing contrast!

# 3. Russia's Move into Palestine

According to Ezekiel 38 and 39, Russia and a group of her allies will one day launch an all-out attack on Israel. They will march their troops onto Jewish soil and encamp in the mountains of Palestine. Just when they are on the verge of success, God will suddenly intervene and their forces will be supernaturally destroyed.

On the surface, these statements may appear to be an attempt to get a hearing by being sensational. I can remember a time that I reacted negatively whenever I heard a minister make these assertions. I actually used the term "claptrap" to describe this teaching in a letter I once wrote. (I hope it's long since been destroyed.) I thought that Bible teachers who applied Ezekiel 38 and 39 to Russia were just letting their prejudices show. After all, the leaders of Russia are atheistic communists and the avowed enemies of Christianity, democracy, and capitalism. It's always nice to find a Bible prophecy that predicts an overwhelming defeat for your foes.

Now, what led me to change my mind? Did I come to distrust and hate the communists so much that I unconsciously began to see Russia and her destruction in these Bible chapters? Not at all! I can truthfully say that I love the Russian people, and I pray for them. My heart goes out to them. How terribly they suffered under the Czars! How bloody their revolution was! How disillusioned they must be today! How difficult it is to be a Christian there!

As I think about the ordinary Russian family, I can't help but pray for them. I ask the Lord to bring about a change of heart in the Russian leaders that will lead them to be kind to Christians, and to negotiate a good arms-limitation agreement with the United States. I hate to hear talk like, "We should have blown Russia off the globe before she developed her own nuclear weapons." And I don't like to hear about hunger anywhere, not even in Russia or other communist countries.

No, I do not hate the Russian people. My belief that Ezekiel 38 and 39 depict a coming disaster for the Soviet Union and her allies does not stem from a feeling of animosity. The reason is this: I don't think these chapters make good sense when interpreted in any other way. You'll see my reasons as you proceed in this chapter. We'll try to identify the nations involved, determine when the Russian move into Palestine will occur, describe the actual invasion, and consider the aftermath of this doomed military expedition.

## IDENTIFICATION OF THE NATIONS INVOLVED

First let's try to establish the identity of the principal nation and her allies in this coming military campaign. We can't be sure about every detail in this prophecy, but we can show positively that Russia and certain countries to the north and east of Israel will be involved.

We begin our study with Ezekiel 38:2, which says, "Son of man, set your face against Gog, of the land of Magog, the chief prince of Meshech and Tubal; prophesy against him and say: 'This is what the Sovereign

Lord says: I am against you, O Gog, chief prince of Meshech and Tubal.' " To determine the nations involved, we will look at the key proper nouns in these verses. They are: Gog, Magog, Meshech, Tubal, and perhaps Rosh. (The Hebrew word translated as "chief" in this verse is the adjective *rosh.* However, this word can also be a proper noun.)

"Gog" is the symbolic name for the leader of the nation that heads the confederation that will invade Palestine. The expression "the land of Magog" denotes a territory about which we have specific information. Dr. C. von Orelli in *The New Schaff-Herzog Encyclopedia* wrote about the Magogites as follows:

A people usually identified with the Scythians. In Genesis 10:2 the second son of Japheth, named Magog, stands between Gomer and Madai. This sets him forth as the representative of a great people, if not of an entire group of nations north of Palestine. . . . a stricter geographical location would place Magog's dwelling between Armenia and Media, perhaps on the shores of the Araxes. But the people seem to have extended farther north across the Caucasus, filling there the extreme northern horizon of the Hebrews (Vol. V, p. 14).

The people who fill this "extreme northern horizon of the Hebrews" are the Russians. One need only consult a world map or globe to be convinced of this. Ezekiel 38:15 declares that it is exactly from this area that the attack against Palestine will originate. "You will come from your place in the *far north,* you and many nations with you." The territory called Magog, therefore, is without question the land now called Russia.

The second proper noun (if we temporarily bypass the word "rosh") is "Meshech." The word "Meshech" (38:2) appears first in the Bible as the name of one of the sons of Japheth. Some scholars claim that it is an ancient tribal name for Moscow. A number of classical historians mention a people called the "Moschi" who lived in the area between the Black Sea and the Caspian Sea. It is possible that these same people came to be known as the Muscovites, and this in turn may be connected with modern Moscow.

The third proper noun, "Tubal," is sometimes linked with present-day Tobolsk in Russia. The well-known Hebrew scholar Gesenius made this connection in his lexicon.

The Hebrew word *rosh* is translated "chief" in many English versions. But Gesenius linked it with Russia. He wrote that it is "the proper name for the northern nation, mentioned with Tubal and Meshech, undoubtedly the Russians, who are mentioned by the Byzantine writers of the tenth century, dwelling to the north of Taurus" (Gesenius, "Hebrew and Chaldee Lexicon").

Although Meshech, Tubal, and Rosh are thus connected with modern Moscow, Tobolsk, and Russia by some language scholars, these identifications are not at all certain. They are based partly upon a thin thread of evidence—that words used centuries ago sound like words used today. The scholars who link Meshech and Tubal with Phyrgia and Cappadocia may be right. In this case they would be close neighbors of the Magogites, the people identified by Josephus as the Scythian tribes who lived in the area we know today as the Soviet Union.

The fact that Magog is positively associated with the territory now belonging to the Soviets, plus the declaration that this leading nation in the invasion will come "from your place in the far north" (38:15), gives us strong evidence for identifying Russia as the leading nation in this prophecy. Because of this, we don't need to make dubious claims about the meaning of Meshech, Tubal, and *rosh.*

The nations joining Magog in this southern march are declared to be Persia, Cush, Put, Gomer, Beth-Togarmah (38:5,6), Sheba, Dedan, and Tarshish (38:13). Persia is modern-day Iran. Cush is Ethiopia. Put is Libya. Gomer is identified as the eastern part of Germany. Beth-Togarmah refers to the Armenians, a people who settled in territory which now belongs to Eastern Turkey, Southern Russia, and Iran. Sheba and

Dedan refer to Arab peoples. Tarshish may be Spain, but we are not certain. It cannot be Great Britian, as some have assumed. All in all, Ezekiel gives us a picture of a great company of soldiers moving southward toward Palestine, the majority of them coming from the area around the Black Sea and Caspian Sea.

## THE TIME OF THE INVASION

When will this Russian-led invasion of Palestine take place? Or has it already happened? On the basis of scriptural evidence, I believe that it will occur near to the time of Christ's return, and I'll explain why.

Before I do, however, I wish to deal with two erroneous ideas about Ezekiel 38 and 39. Some Bible students say that the prophecies of these chapters have already been fulfilled. But if they are asked when, they are in trouble, for they cannot point to a historical event that even remotely resembles what Ezekiel wrote. Some scholars recognize this problem, but they get around it by saying that Ezekiel 38 and 39 are a "prophetic parable." They define this as a prophecy that must not be interpreted in a literal, historical manner. They are very vague, however, when asked to define what the term "prophetic parable" means. Neither can they explain its purpose. Nor can they point to one word in these chapters which indicates that the prophecies are to be taken as symbolic statements.

The predictions of Ezekiel 38 and 39 are written exactly like the other prophetic portions of the Old Testament. Many of these other prophecies have already been fulfilled—and literally. We believe that those which have not been realized will also be literally fulfilled in the future. This holds true for Ezekiel 38 and 39 as well. The prophet declared that the events he depicted will take place "in days to come" (38:16), and at a time when the Israelites in Palestine feel secure and unthreatened. Ezekiel as God's spokesman addressed Gog, the leader of Magog, as follows:

*Get ready; be prepared, you and all the hordes*
*gathered about you, and take command of them. After*

*many days you will be called to arms. In future years*
*you will invade a land that has recovered from war,*
*whose people were gathered from many nations to the*
*mountains of Israel, which had long been desolate.*
*They had been brought out from the nations, and now*
*all of them live in safety. You and all your troops and*
*the many nations with you will go up, advancing like a*
*storm; you will be like a cloud covering the land.*

*This is what the Sovereign Lord says: On that day*
*thoughts will come into your mind and you will devise*
*an evil scheme. You will say, "I will invade a land of*
*unwalled villages; I will attack a peaceful and*
*unsuspecting people—all of them living without walls*
*and without gates and bars. I will plunder and loot and*
*turn my hand against the resettled ruins and the people*
*gathered from the nations, rich in livestock and goods,*
*living at the center of the land" (Ezekiel 38:7-12).*

Obviously, the peaceful conditions expressed in these
words do not exist today. Yes, Israel is a nation in
Palestine. In perfect harmony with the "dry bones"
prophecy of Ezekiel 37, a great number of Jewish
people have returned to their homeland. But they certainly are not living in peace and security. They are
surrounded by enemies. Their armies are battle-ready.

By all appearances, Israel will maintain top military
readiness until some powerful ruler of a strong confederacy of nations guarantees that he will protect her
and secure the cooperation of her neighbors. In the
preceding chapter we pointed out that Daniel 9:26,27
teaches that this is precisely what is going to happen. A
strong Western ruler will make a 7-year pact with
Israel, only to turn abruptly against her halfway
through the agreement. During this brief 42-month
period of apparent security in Israel, Russia and her
allies will launch the attack against Israel described in
Ezekiel 38 and 39.

Will Christians be raptured before the Russian confederacy marches into Palestine? I don't know. The
rapture is an imminent event; it could occur today.
And the Bible doesn't tell us whether it will take place

before this 7-year pact is made or shortly afterward. The great tribulation will begin when Antichrist starts his bitter persecution of all who turn to God. We know the church will be raptured before this terrible time begins, but we don't know whether it will be several years or a few days beforehand. This is why, while not ignoring the "signs of the times," we should be ready for the Lord's any-moment return.

## THE INVASION DESCRIBED

Motivated by greed, the armies from the north will begin to move southward toward Palestine—not knowing that they are walking into a trap God has set for them, and that they will be destroyed. Ezekiel wrote:

> Therefore, son of man, prophesy and say to Gog: This is what the Sovereign Lord says: In that day, when My people Israel are living in safety, will you not take notice of it? You will come from your place in the far north, you and many nations with you, all of them riding on horses, a great horde, a mighty army. You will advance against My people Israel like a cloud that covers the land. In days to come, O Gog, I will bring you against My land, so that the nations may know Me when I show Myself holy through you before their eyes.
>
> This is what the Sovereign Lord says: Are you not the one I spoke of in former days by My servants the prophets of Israel? At that time they prophesied for years that I would bring you against them. This is what will happen in that day: When Gog attacks the land of Israel, My hot anger will be aroused, declares the Sovereign Lord. In My zeal and fiery wrath I declare that at that time there shall be a great earthquake in the land of Israel. The fish of the sea, the birds of the air, the beasts of the field, every creature that moves along the ground, and all the people on the face of the earth will tremble at My presence. The mountains will be overturned, the cliffs will crumble and every wall will fall to the ground. I will summon a sword against Gog on all My mountains, declares the Sovereign Lord. Every man's sword will be against his brother.

*I will execute judgment upon him with plague and
bloodshed; I will pour down torrents of rain, hailstones and burning sulfur on him and on his troops and
on the many nations with him. And so I will show My
greatness and My holiness, and I will make Myself
known in the sight of many nations. Then they will
know that I am the Lord (Ezekiel 38:14-23).*

The Lord will be angry with these nations for their unbelief and wickedness, and He will use their invasion of
Palestine to punish them. In going against Israel, they
will be attacking "God's people" and God's "land" (see
vv. 14,16). His fierce retribution will fall upon them
while they are encamped in the mountains of Judea.

As I write these words, the Israelites themselves are
still unrepentant and rebellious. They fulfill the condition expressed by the Lord through His prophet Hosea,
"Call him [Gomer's third son] Lo-Ammi, for you are not
My people, and I am not your God" (1:9).

Even so, God is watching over His people Israel. He
hasn't abandoned them. He will take up again His special dealing with them when Antichrist makes his firm
agreement with Israel. This will begin the "seventieth
'seven'" (Daniel 9:26,27), and will cause God to display
openly His wrath against Israel's enemies. As soon as
the northern invaders, coming down in separate
droves, reach certain specified places in Palestine, they
will be thrown into a panic by a tremendous
earthquake, torrents of rain, huge hailstones, and burning sulphur. In their consternation they will become
totally disorganized, seeking personal safety with such
wild terror that they will kill one another. As a result,
their dead bodies will cover the landscape and become
the prey of scavenger birds and beasts.

The leaders in Russia and other communist countries
deny God's existence. Most of the Arab peoples reject
the Jehovah of the Bible and His Son. They hate the
nation of Israel and will attempt to plunder her, perhaps destroy her. But the tables will be turned. They
will be defeated and broken by the intervening hand of
Almighty God.

## THE AFTERMATH
## OF GOD'S INTERVENTION

After Ezekiel described God's overwhelming judgment upon the invaders, he depicted three elements that will be part of the outcome of this dramatic and awesome event. First, people all over the earth will be astounded at the defeat of these powerful armies, and they will acknowledge God's power (39:7,8). Second, the inhabitants of Israel will use the wreckage on the battlefield for fuel for many years (39:9,10). Third, the Israelites will be occupied with disposing of the dead bodies of the slain for a period of 7 months (39:12-15). We will consider each of these consequences, but in reverse order.

*The Extended Burial Time*

The prophet declared that a period of 7 months will elapse before the task of burying the dead is completed.

> *For seven months the house of Israel will be burying them in order to cleanse the land. All the people of the land will bury them, and the day I am glorified will be a memorable day for them, declares the Sovereign Lord.*
>
> *Men will be regularly employed to cleanse the land. Some will go throughout the land and, in addition to them, others will bury those that remain on the ground. At the end of the seven months they will begin their search. As they go through the land and one of them sees a human bone, he will set up a marker beside it until the gravediggers have buried it in the Valley of Hamon Gog (Ezekiel 39:12-15).*

This will be a burial of the bones of the dead soldiers, not their corpses. The prophecy tells us that scavenger birds and carnivorous animals will eat the flesh. The rapid decomposition process brought on by the climate in Palestine will quickly complete the job.

The critics contend that 7 months to complete the burial seems like quite a long time. They point out that according to verse 13 "all the people of the land" will be involved in the burying task, and they declare that a literal interpretation of this passage means that the dead would number at least 360 million. They arrive at this figure by tabulating the results of one million people working at the task 6 days a week, with each burying two corpses daily. But the text doesn't say that a million people will work at this undertaking. The stench will be so bad that only a few men wearing masks can start. Then, after the odor of death and decay has subsided, others will be able to go in. Later everyone could be involved in the process suggested in verse 15. As they travel through the land, wherever they see a human bone, they will set up a marker as a guide to the burial crew. I don't view Ezekiel's declaration that a total of 7 months will be occupied in disposing of the dead as a reason for not interpreting this prophecy in a literal way.

### The Burning of the Weapons

Another element in the aftermath of this carnage will be the use of the wreckage by the Israelites for fuel.

*Then those who live in the towns of Israel will go out and use the weapons for fuel and burn them up—the small and large shields, the bows and arrows, the war clubs and spears. For seven years they will use them for fuel. They will not need to gather wood from the fields or cut it from the forests, because they will use the weapons for fuel. And they will plunder those who plundered them and loot those who looted them, declares the Sovereign Lord (Ezekiel 39:9,10).*

The first problem the critics raise is this: Why will a country like Russia, which possesses highly sophisticated weapons, resort to using the kind of equipment described here—small and large shields, bows and arrows, war clubs and spears? The answer is simple: God gave this vision to a man who had never heard of an airplane or a tank or a gun. The prophet would have been totally confused if the Lord had shown him these modern weapons. Therefore, God gave him the picture of a well-equipped and mobile army in terms that made sense to the prophet and to the people who would hear him speak or read his words.

The second question is: How will the Israelites be

able to use wrecked modern war equipment for fuel? Iron doesn't burn very well. True—but gasoline and diesel fuel do. Moreover, it is reported that some European countries have developed a new material that is strong as steel, rustproof, and can easily be cut into sections with blowtorches. Furthermore, it is combustible when exposed to open flames. Of course, we can't declare dogmatically that the northern nations will use weapons made of this material—but neither can we be sure they won't. A detail like this should not make us shy away from a literal interpretation of this passage. A study of prophecy that is already fulfilled shows us that the Lord performed the "impossible" time and again to bring to pass what He had declared.

### Divine Acknowledgment

The third aftermath of this supernatural devastation of Palestine's northern enemies is a worldwide acknowledgment of God's existence and of His special concern for Israel. This will undoubtedly be a factor in the conversion of great multitudes of Jews and Gentiles, many of whom will suffer and die for their faith during the great tribulation (Revelation 6:9-11;7:9-17;13:5-18). Here is Ezekiel's description of the spiritual aftermath:

> I will make known My holy name among My people Israel. I will no longer let My holy name be profaned, and the nations will know that I the Lord am the Holy One in Israel.
>
> I will display My glory among the nations, and all the nations will see the punishment I inflict and the hand I lay upon them. From that day forward the house of Israel will know that I am the Lord their God. And the nations will know that the people of Israel went into exile for their sin, because they were unfaithful to Me. So I hid My face from them and handed them over to their enemies, and they all fell by the sword. I dealt with them according to their uncleanness and their offenses, and I hid My face from them.
>
> Therefore this is what the Sovereign Lord says: I will

*now bring Jacob back from captivity and will have*
*compassion on all the people of Israel, and I will be*
*zealous for My holy name. They will forget their shame*
*and all the unfaithfulness they showed toward Me*
*when they lived in safety in their land with no one to*
*make them afraid. When I have brought them back*
*from the nations and have gathered them from the*
*countries of their enemies, I will show Myself holy*
*through them in the sight of many nations. Then they*
*will know that I am the Lord their God, for though I*
*sent them into exile among the nations, I will gather*
*them to their own land, not leaving any behind. I will no*
*longer hide My face from them, for I will pour out My*
*Spirit on the house of Israel, declares the Sovereign*
*Lord (Ezekiel 39:7,21-29).*

Jews and Gentiles all over the world will recognize that
the Lord did indeed intervene on Israel's behalf. They
will view their miraculous deliverance as a signal that
God has once again placed them in the center of His
program. They will understand that the Jews were
scattered because, as God Himself put it, "I hid My face
from them." This will lead many to repentance. Those
who turn to God through Jesus Christ will be forced to
flee, and they will be in constant danger of death
because of persecution by Antichrist. But these
faithful believers will anticipate the fulfillment of this
promise of Jehovah: "I will now bring Jacob back from
captivity and will have compassion on all the people of
Israel, and I will be zealous for My holy name" (39:25).

Russia's defeat may be the catalyst that brings
about Antichrist's turning against the Jews, but it will
also be the beginning of Israel's conversion. This will
result in Christ's glorious return and the complete
restoration of Israel. Their long history of rebellion and
suffering will then be ended. The Lord summed up the
whole story in this message to Ezekiel:

*Son of man, when the people of Israel were living in*
*their own land, they defiled it by their conduct and their*
*actions.... So I poured out My wrath on them....*
*I dispersed them among the nations.... And wherever*

*they went among the nations they profaned My holy
name. . . .*

*Therefore say to the house of Israel, 'This is what the
sovereign Lord says: It is not for your sake, O house of
Israel, that I am going to do these things, but for the
sake of My holy name, which you have profaned among
the nations where you have gone (Ezekiel 36:17-20,22).*

Israel's "seventieth 'seven'" will begin when Antichrist, the ruler of a Western confederacy of nations,
makes a 7-year treaty with them. When he does, God
will initiate His program for the conversion and
restoration of Israel. During the great tribulation,
which begins halfway through this treaty when the
Western ruler turns against the Jews, Israel will turn
to Christ as their true Messiah. One of the factors
leading to this spiritual renewal will be the
supernatural defeat of Russia sometime during the
first half of this 7-year span.

# 4. The Roman Empire Restored

I'm sure you've heard the reports that the European Common Market is a sign of Christ's return. I believe it well may be just that!

The Common Market is a group of Western European countries formed to improve the financial status of their citizens. Geographically, these nations cover a significant portion of the area once included in the Roman Empire. This is of keen interest to Bible students, because the visions recorded in Daniel 2 and 7 teach that a Western confederation of ten nations will be in existence when Jesus Christ returns in glory. We will get the clearest picture of the restoration of the Roman Empire by taking a careful look at Daniel 2 and relating it to Revelation 13.

## DANIEL 2

The revived Roman Empire first appears in the interpretation of Nebuchadnezzar's dream recorded in the book of Daniel, chapter 2. The king saw a large statue, its head of pure gold, its chest and arms of silver, its belly and thighs of bronze, its legs of iron, and its feet partly of iron and partly of baked clay. While he was looking at it, a rock—mysteriously cut out of a mountain—rolled down the mountain, struck the statue on its feet of iron and clay, and smashed it to bits. The entire image was so pulverized that it was blown away like chaff (see Daniel 2:31-35).

When the king awoke, he had forgotten his dream. His astrologers couldn't tell him what he had dreamed, much less what the dream meant, so they had to step aside for Daniel. God's servant told Nebuchadnezzar that he was represented by the head of gold, and that the other sections in the image symbolized three succeeding powerful kingdoms. A study of the Bible and secular history combine to inform us that they were Medo-Persia, Greece, and Rome. The same empires are presented in Daniel 7 under the figure of a lion, a bear, a leopard, and a terrible beast. Each of these four empires appeared on the scene and passed away. Rome lasted the longest, but it gradually deteriorated until it was divided into two sections—the western part coming to its end in A.D. 476 and the eastern half continuing until about 1453.

Nebuchadnezzar's vision portrayed a rock smiting the image in the feet and blowing the whole image to bits. That sudden end and total destruction never came upon Babylon, Medo-Persia, Greece, or Rome. The "rock cut out of a mountain" represents Christ at His return. This is acknowledged by almost all conservative Bible scholars. He is the One who will destroy the image. Therefore, we can only conclude that the Roman Empire will be restored. Here is what Daniel said:

*In the time of those kings [represented by the ten toes of the feet], the God of heaven will set up a kingdom that will never be destroyed, nor will it be left to another people. It will crush all those kingdoms and bring them to an end, but it will itself endure forever. This is the meaning of the vision of the rock cut out of a mountain, but not by human hands—a rock that broke the iron, the bronze, the clay, the silver, and the gold to pieces (Daniel 2:44,45).*

Although the Roman Empire gradually came to an end, it left some remnants of its genius. The *Corpus Juris Civilis* (body of Roman law) remains as the basis of jurisprudence throughout the Western World. Latin continues to be the technical language in science and medicine. The Bible tells us that the Roman Empire will be revived about the time Antichrist gains control of the Western World.

A number of questions are asked when someone mentions the revived Roman Empire. What about the boundaries of this new empire? Will they be similar to those of the great Roman Empire of the past? Will its capital again be Rome?

In answer, let me point out that an empire can maintain its identity even though its boundaries may fluctuate. The British Empire continued to be the British Empire for a long time—during a period of strong growth and a later period of gradual decline. An empire can even change capitals without losing its identity. Erich Sauer wrote: "China remained China though its capital was removed from Peking to Nanking, some 570 miles south. Russia remained Russia though its capital was no longer St. Petersburg but, as now, Moscow. Or, to take an example from the history of western Europe, England has remained England though originally its capital was not London but, in the days of the old Saxon kings, Winchester, ... and London became the capital only in the 13th century. Similarly, the fourth empire of Daniel will remain the same empire even if, in the final development, not the literal Rome, that is, its first capital, but some other city should become the capital." *(The Triumph of the Crucified,* Eerdmans, 1951, p. 134.)

Yes, the Roman Empire will be revived—though not necessarily with the exact boundaries of the past or with Rome as its capital. Even so, it will be generally associated with the ancient empire. The European Common Market, therefore, could have great significance. It may be a sign that we are not far removed from the end of our age. It might even be the first step in God's program leading to the restoration of the Roman Empire under Antichrist. In any event, the Bible teaches that it will be destroyed by Jesus Christ at His return.

## REVELATION 13

The restored Roman Empire is pictured symbolically in Revelation 13 as a beast with seven heads and ten horns. It has the general appearance of a leopard, the feet of a bear, and the mouth of a lion.

*And I saw a beast coming out of the sea. He had ten horns and seven heads, with ten crowns on his horns, and on each head a blasphemous name. The beast I saw resembled a leopard, but had feet like those of a bear and a mouth like that of a lion. The dragon gave the beast his power and his throne and great authority (Revelation 13:1,2).*

Now, a ten-horned, seven-headed creature with a leopard-like body, bear-like paws, and a lion-like mouth would be quite a monstrosity. But we must remember that this is symbolism. Each item in this description tells us something different about the end-time empire of Antichrist.

Let's begin by considering the seven heads and ten horns. Six of the heads, I believe, represent the great kingdoms of Bible history—Egypt, Assyria, Babylon, Medo-Persia, Greece, and Rome. The seventh is the Roman Empire in its restored form. The ten horns represent the ten nations which will form the nucleus of Antichrist's empire. In Revelation 17:12 these horns are declared to be "ten kings who have not yet received a kingdom, but who for one hour will receive authority as kings along with the beast." They have the same symbolic meaning as the ten toes of the image in Nebuchadnezzar's dream (Daniel 2).

The beast is also said to have the general appearance of a leopard, the paws of a bear, and the mouth of a lion. The meaning of these figurative elements is not difficult to determine. Daniel 7 portrays Babylon as a lion, Medo-Persia as a bear, and Greece as a leopard. Thus we conclude that the kingdom of Antichrist will combine the strongest attributes of the great empires of the past. The seven heads and the three animal symbols combine to show us that everything great about Egypt, Assyria, Babylon, Medo-Persia, Greece, and Rome will be present in the restored Roman Empire.

The apostle John said that one head will apparently die from a serious wound, but that he will be brought back to life. We read:

> *One of the heads of the beast seemed to have had a fatal wound, but the fatal wound had been healed. The whole world was astonished and followed the beast (Revelation 13:3).*

This verse has led many Bible students to speculate that Antichrist may be a wicked man from history who will be brought back from the dead. Some of the names mentioned are Antiochus Epiphanes, Nero, Caesar, Judas Iscariot, Napoleon, and Hitler. Some students of prophecy have had a good time trying to figure out who it might be by working with the number 666, which is mentioned at the close of Revelation 13 as "the number of the beast." By assigning a number value to the letters of the Hebrew, Greek, and Roman alphabets, they have come up with a large array of prominent personalities, past and present, as candidates for the role of Antichrist.

These speculations are futile and a waste of time for at least two reasons. First, the "wounded head" should be related to Antichrist's empire, not his person. The revival of the empire is what causes the consternation, not the return of a man to life. Second, we might as well quit trying to find a deep and mysterious meaning for 666. It probably simply means that even though Satan tries to imitate the Triune Godhead, all three members of his counterfeit "trinity" come short of the perfection of God, which is denoted by the number 7. Besides, we won't know exactly how this number will be used in the "mark of the beast," no matter how many guesses we make.

In summary, the Bible teaches clearly that the

Roman Empire will be restored. But we cannot be sure about the specifics. The capital city may be Rome, or it may be Babylon on the Euphrates. The territory it covers may involve only Europe, or it may extend to North America. We cannot settle these matters with certainty. In fact, they will not become clear until the Lord fulfills the prophecies. As God's servants, we have far more important things to do than occupy our minds with vain speculations. We will bring more glory to Christ by serving Him with all our strength, leaving unrevealed endtime matters to Him.

# 5. *The Great Tribulation*

In spite of energy and pollution problems, severe recessions, international tensions, and alarming crime statistics, some people continue to paint a glowing picture of the future. They refuse to face the possibility of a nuclear war, saying that the outcome is so terrible to contemplate that no one would ever think of starting one. They are unmoved by the shortage in energy and increase in pollution, declaring that the sun and hydrogen will soon provide mankind with an unlimited supply of clean fuel. They have unbounded confidence that new hybrids in agriculture and advances in weather control will eliminate food shortages. They envision the third world nations developing their own resources and improving their technology until they reach a high level of economic prosperity.

Most thinking people, however, do not share this ardently optimistic view of the future. They are afraid that an irrational leader somewhere will set off a nuclear exchange. They are convinced that many people now living in affluence will soon find it necessary to lower their standard of living. Meteorologists are fearful that pollution in the upper atmosphere may do freakish

51

things to the weather and bring about mass starvation. Yes, I am amazed at the number of thinking people, many of them non-Christians, who believe that the end of our civilization is at hand.

Regarding the future, I am neither an unbounded optimist nor a gloomy pessimist. While I am positive about eternity, I have some serious misgivings about the immediate future. Man's moral development, for example, has by no means kept pace with his technological advances. In fact, people are just as immoral, selfish, and cruel as ever. The human race with its nuclear weapons resembles a child playing with a loaded gun. Sometime or another it could go off, bringing worldwide disaster.

I am not about to resign myself, however, to being destroyed in a nuclear holocaust. I have good reason for saying this, because I believe the rapture of the church could take place at any moment. Besides that, I'm not convinced that God is going to allow an all-out nuclear exchange in the near future. In fact, it could be that neither the rapture nor a nuclear war will take place during the present generation. God may see fit to give us a period of relative peace and prosperity. He could respond to the prayers of His people and bring about a great spiritual awakening among believers, and this in turn could reverse the moral climate all over the world.

Let me hasten to point out that, whether things get better or worse, a period of terrible tribulation is inevitable. The Scriptures make it clear that intense devastation and terror will sweep over the earth just before Jesus Christ returns to establish His kingdom. Bible-believing Christians in both amillennial and premillennial circles agree that a period of unparalleled distress awaits mankind. Some say that believers will go through it, while others are convinced that the church will be raptured first. They concur, however, in their conviction that the tribulation will take place.

In this chapter I want to trace the course of that unprecedented time of terrible trouble and suffering we call the tribulation. I will do so by focusing upon its unpleasant elements—revolution, famine, pestilence, demonic affliction, and natural disasters. The positive factors of the tribulation will be considered later.

The primary teaching on the great tribulation is given to us in the book of Revelation. It is portrayed by three distinct symbols—seals, trumpets, and bowls of wrath. The seals will be opened by Jesus Himself as He reclaims the earth from Satan's domination. Angels will blow the trumpets and empty the bowls of God's wrath. The events associated with the seals, trumpets, and bowls occur during a timespan of 3 and 1/2 years.

I believe the seal judgments will take place over the entire 3 and 1/2 year period. The trumpet judgments will begin at some undesignated point within it. The bowl judgments will be poured out in rapid succession during the closing weeks. The well-known amillennial scholar William Hendriksen presented this structure in his commentary on the book of Revelation, referring to it as "progressive parallelism." My view may be represented as follows:

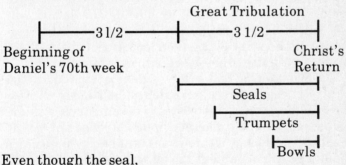

Even though the seal,
trumpet, and bowl judgments
will begin at different times, they
will all come to an end at the glorious return of Christ.

## THE SEVEN SEALS (Revelation 6:1-17)

The apostle John's inspired description of the great tribulation began with his portrayal of Jesus opening a seven-sealed scroll. As the seals were broken and the scroll was unrolled, great events came into focus. The process gave John a bird's-eye view of the entire 3 and 1/2 year period we call "the great tribulation."

*The Rider on the White Horse* (Revelation 6:1,2). When the first seal was opened by Christ, a rider on a white horse burst into view. The color of the steed signifies victory in battle, the bow in the warrior's hand symbolizes his control of the weapons of warfare, and the crown on his head depicts his acknowledged position of authority. This rider is Antichrist! He will come upon the world scene in a time of general distress, and he will appear to be the hope of mankind.

*The Rider on the Red Horse* (Revelation 6:3,4). The breaking of the second seal brings before us the same rider, but this time he is on a red horse. This color symbolizes bloodshed and war. We are told that the horseman has "power to take peace from the earth and to make men slay each other." Furthermore, he "was given a large sword."

We have seen from our study of Antichrist that when he feels his position is secure he will instigate a program of cruel persecution against the Jews. Violence begets violence; therefore, worldwide revolution will soon follow. These conflicts will escalate until they culminate in the war of Armageddon. Antichrist will not fulfill his promise to bring peace to mankind.

*The Rider on the Black Horse* (Revelation 6:5,6). The opening of the third seal revealed a black horse with its rider holding a pair of scales. His entrance was accompanied by the announcement, "A quart of wheat for a day's wages, and three quarts of barley for a day's wages, and do not damage the oil and the wine!"

This black horse with its rider symbolizes famine. During the tribulation, food will become so scarce that it will have to be weighed out carefully. Prices will be so high that a man will have to work a whole day for one ration of wheat or three rations of barley. The supply of "oil and wine," however, will not diminish. This indicates that the rich will still be able to buy their luxury foods, even while the poor go hungry. The sad old story of the rich getting richer and the poor getting poorer will continue—in spite of Antichrist's promise of prosperity for all.

*The Rider on the Pale Horse* (Revelation 6:7,8). While John looked on, the fourth seal was opened and a pale, greenish-colored horse appeared. Its rider was named Death. He was followed closely by Hades, the abode of the dead.

The coming of the rider on the pale horse indicates the intensity of the suffering under the red and black horses. We are told that one-fourth of the earth's population will be killed "by sword, famine and plague, and by the wild beasts of the earth." The two new elements that will bring death under the symbolism of this horse are "plague," and "the wild beasts of the earth."

Violence, famine, disease, and "the wild beasts of the earth" will bring death to multitudes in the great tribulation. The word "beasts" may refer to cruel and wicked men. Remember, Antichrist and the False Prophet are portrayed as beasts in Revelation 13. If we take the expression "wild beasts" literally, though, we can only conjecture about how this prophecy will be fulfilled. Earthquakes may bring about the release of hundreds of zoo animals. Wild with hunger brought on by the food shortage, they could slay many people.

The declaration that one-fourth of the world's population will die staggers the imagination. Right now, that would be more than one billion people! Later we'll see that another vast multitude will be killed by the demonic hordes described in Revelation 9.

*The Souls under the Altar* (Revelation 6:9-11). When the Lamb opened the fifth seal, John saw "under the altar the souls of those who had been slain because of the word of God and the testimony they had maintained" (v. 9). These martyrs were calling upon God to avenge their deaths. He answered by giving them white robes. (This implies that believers will possess form or substance during the intermediate state.) The Lord then told these martyrs that they were to wait a little longer, until all the saints marked out for martyrdom had been killed.

These souls under the altar represent believers who will die during the great tribulation. (Remember, the saints of the church age will already have been raptured and will possess their resurrection bodies.) Many people will turn to Christ during the tribulation, and they will die for their faith because they refuse to worship the beast or his image. This same group is mentioned in Revelation 7:9-17, where they are seen in white robes and are heard to cry out, "Salvation belongs to our God, who sits on the throne, and to the Lamb" (v. 10). We will discuss salvation during the great tribulation in the next chapter.

*Final Events* (Revelation 6:12-17). When the sixth seal was opened, John saw a great earthquake rock our planet. In addition, the sun turned black, the moon became blood-red, stars fell to the earth, the sky rolled up like a scroll, and mountains and islands disappeared. When these cataclysmic events take place, raw terror will grip the ungodly. Having rejected the Almighty, they will irrationally call on the mountains and rocks, crying out, "Fall on us and hide us from the face of Him who sits on the throne and from the wrath of the Lamb! For the great day of their wrath has come, and who can stand?" (vv. 16,17).

The events here resemble the picture of the great tribulation's close described by Jesus in the Olivet Discourse:

*Immediately after the distress of those days the sun will be darkened, and the moon will not give its light; the stars will fall from the sky, and the heavenly bodies will be shaken.*

*At that time the sign of the Son of Man will appear in the sky, and all the nations of the earth will mourn. They will see the Son of Man coming on the clouds of the sky, with power and great glory. And He will send His angels with a loud trumpet call, and they will gather His elect from the four winds, from one end of the heavens to the other (Matthew 24:29-31).*

Hal Lindsay captioned this event, "The First Nuclear Exchange," saying that it will happen somewhere near the middle of Daniel's 70th week. He pointed out that nuclear bombs make the earth shake, and that the contamination they bring into the atmosphere could well make the sun appear to be blood-red. He added that nuclear-tipped missiles may take on the appearance of meteors falling from heaven, and he speculated that the atmosphere doubling back on itself after a nuclear explosion may resemble a rolling up of the sky.

I disagree with his conclusions. In a nuclear exchange, it seems highly unlikely that people close enough to see it would be able to cry out to the mountains and rocks. They'd be vaporized or seared. Moreover, unbelievers during the first part of Daniel's 70th week (where Lindsay places this event) would not necessarily associate a nuclear attack with the wrath of the Lamb. It seems to me that this passage makes far better sense when we view it as paralleling Matthew 24:29-31 and occurring at the close of the tribulation.

## THE SEVEN TRUMPETS (Revelation 8,9,11)

The opening of the seventh seal brought into view seven angels with trumpets. When each trumpet was sounded, the apostle saw another fierce judgment come upon the earth. These events will be terribly severe—so awesome that when the seventh seal is opened in preparation for them, heaven is quiet for about half an hour (see Revelation 8:1). Remember, the events we see symbolized under these trumpet judgments will take place during the great tribulation, while the earth is being plagued with revolution, persecution, famines, disease, and the other death-dealing phenomena depicted under the first six seals.

*Hail and Fire* (Revelation 8:7). At some point during the great tribulation, an outpouring of what looks like hail and fire mixed with blood will destroy a third of the trees on earth. All the green grass will die. This complete destruction will likely include food grains such as wheat, oats, and barley, and it will no doubt intensify the worldwide food shortage.

*A Burning Mountain Falls* (Revelation 8:8,9). With

the blowing of the second trumpet, a huge burning mass that looks like a mountain will fall from heaven and plunge into the sea. One-third of the marine life and one-third of all ships will be destroyed. Note that John didn't say it was a burning mountain—only that it had the appearance of one. Perhaps it will be a large meteor. The destruction will not be worldwide but limited to the area where the falling object will land.

*A Star Like a Burning Lamp* (Revelation 8:10,11). The blowing of the third trumpet brought to John's vision a large, flaming star falling from the sky. It will explode into bits, contaminating one-third of mankind's fresh water supply.

*The Lights Go Out* (Revelation 8:12,13). When the fourth trumpet blows, a strange, intermittent darkening of the heavenly bodies will take place. During the daylight period, the earth will not receive the light of the sun for 4 hours; during the night, the moon and stars will be hidden 4 hours.

The judgments of the first four trumpets will involve the natural world—trees, grass, water, and light. Some Bible scholars contend that these are depictions of three nuclear explosions and their aftermath. The sky will be so darkened by the blast, they say, that a third of the light that comes from the sun, moon, and stars will be shut off. This is possible, but I think it is highly unlikely. It seems to me that these are supernatural judgments from heaven. I believe they are designed to show mankind that God is directly involved in the dreaded happenings that will make life on earth almost unbearable during the great tribulation. We are not told at what point of the 3 and 1/2-year tribulation period they will begin, but the nature of these judgments is such that I feel they will be reserved for the final year.

*Locust-like Demons* (Revelation 9:1-12). When the angel in heaven sounded the fifth trumpet, John saw in his vision a fallen star (apparently representing either Satan or another evil angel) receive the key to the bottomless pit and open it. Black smoke issued from the mouth of the abyss, and from this smoke a host of locust-like creatures emerged. They are described as having the general shape of horses, but with faces like men, hair like women, and feet like lions. They are also depicted as having wings, and a tail like a scorpion.

These beings are a special group of demons so evil and vicious that they had been cast into the abyss for the protection of mankind. They will be released at some point rather late in the great tribulation period. Because they are demons, they will not have physical bodies. Therefore, I can't agree with Bible students who teach that these are real locusts which will fly around and sting people. Much less do I agree with a popular writer who suggests that these are Cobra helicopters spraying nerve gas from their tailguns.

These evil spirits will be invisible to mankind. The physical characteristics ascribed to them in John's vision are symbols of their inner or essential characteristics. The declaration that they are commanded not to eat grass and leaves as locusts normally do simply adds to the symbolism. They will inflict sharp pain that resembles the sting of a scorpion, and the aftermath will be 5 months of intense pain. Because the gospels tell us of instances of evil spirits afflicting people with physical ailments, we should not think this to be strange or impossible. Suddenly and unexplainably, many people will cry out because they feel a hot sting. The pain will stay with them for 5 months, and it will be so severe that the people afflicted will wish they could die.

*Two Hundred Million Death-dealing Demons* (Revelation 9:13-21). The sounding of the sixth trumpet will signal the release of 200 million fierce demons. They will kill one-third of mankind. Four evil angels whom God has kept bound at the Euphrates, the boundary line between the East and the West, will be released at the precise moment God has determined in His plan. From the time the Lord bound these angels, He had in mind the time He would release them. That's the meaning of the expression that they "had been kept ready for this very hour and day and month and year" (v. 15). These wicked angels will mobilize an army of 200 million followers, who are portrayed as riding on horses and as having heads like lions and tails like serpents. From their mouths they will belch forth fire, smoke, and sulphur. With their tails, which will be like snakes and have heads, they will bite people. They will kill a third of the human race.

Quite a few Bible scholars, connecting this passage with the "kings of the east" of Revelation 16:12, see these 200 million soldiers as representing an army from China. They say that this great army will move toward the Middle East, destroying great population centers in India, Japan, Pakistan, Indo-China, and Indonesia on their way. Some even suggest that the horses which blow fire, smoke, and sulphur from their mouths represent missile launchers.

I have a difficult time accepting the idea that these 200 million horsemen will be soldiers from China. It seems to me that they will be demons. The general picture is very similar to that depicted in the first 13 verses of this chapter. The primary difference is that these demons will have the power to kill people, not merely to give them 5 months of pain.

We must keep in mind that John is giving us truth through symbols. People on earth will not really see horses with fiery red, dark blue, and yellow breast-plates, lions' heads, and serpent-like tails. These characteristics are given to impress upon the reader the essential nature of these evil spirits who will kill one-third of the human race.

The release of these cruel and powerful evil beings will occur near the close of the great tribulation. People who have not repented up to this point will no longer be able to. We read, "The rest of mankind that were not killed by these plagues still did not repent of the work of their hands; they did not stop worshiping demons, and idols of gold, silver, bronze, stone and wood—idols that cannot see or hear or walk. Nor did they repent of their murders, their magic arts, their sexual immorality or their thefts" (Revelation 9:20,21).

The four sins here mentioned—murder, magic arts, fornication, and theft—are prominent transgressions of our time. They are the natural companions of the life-view of the secular humanists, who have a low regard for human worth. Since fetuses are seen as meaningless blobs, they reason, why not promote abortion-on-demand and mercy-killings? This in turn leads the populace to think lightly of all killing. Then too, when people have no faith and turn to drugs in an effort to find some meaning in life, they often put themselves in touch with demons. This leads to the occult and spiritism. In addition, a lack of respect for human life brings on sexual promiscuity. When life itself isn't viewed as sacred, neither is the marriage relationship. Finally, when persons are seen as having no real value, they have no rights. If you can't get what you want any other way, why not steal it? At the close of the great tribulation, mankind will reap the final harvest of the life-view of the secular humanists.

*The Anticipated Kingdom* (Revelation 11:15-19). With the sounding of the seventh trumpet, John heard a great symphony of voices in heaven declaring, "The kingdom of the world has become the kingdom of our Lord and of His Christ, and He will reign for ever and ever." Then he saw the 24 elders fall to their faces and worship God. They will praise Him because He has punished the evildoers in His wrath and because they will see Him reward His faithful servants.

But this glimpse of the anticipated kingdom is not the complete message of the seventh trumpet. It also announces the devastating bowl judgments which will mark the closing days of the great tribulation.

*Then God's temple in heaven was opened, and within His temple was seen the ark of His covenant. And there came flashes of lightning, rumblings, peals of thunder, an earthquake and a great hailstorm (Revelation 11:19).*

The lightnings, voices, thunderings, earthquake, and hail that accompany the opening of the temple of God in heaven are portrayals of the most severe of the great tribulation judgments, the ones reserved for its final months.

## THE SEVEN BOWLS OF GOD'S WRATH

As noted earlier, the opening of the first six seals gave us a picture of the great tribulation from beginning to end—the entire 3 and 1/2-year span. With the opening of the seventh seal, we saw a series of judgments associated with seven trumpets, disasters which probably will begin as the great tribulation is about to enter its last year. Now we are going to see the outpouring of the seven bowls of God's wrath—judgments that come out of the seventh trumpet and will likely fall upon earth during the final months of this awesome 3 and 1/2-year period. They will occur in rapid succession as the most terrible period in human history draws to a close. When these judgments begin, the people will realize that the time of trouble is almost over. This is beautifully depicted in the following passage:

*I saw in heaven another great and marvelous sign: seven angels with the seven last plagues—last, because with them God's wrath is completed. And I saw what looked like a sea of glass mixed with fire and, standing beside the sea, those who had been victorious over the beast and his image and over the number of his name. They held harps given them by God and sang the song of Moses the servant of God and the song of the Lamb:*

*Great and marvelous are Your deeds, Lord God Almighty. Just and true are Your ways, King of the ages. Who will not fear You, O Lord, and bring glory to Your name? For You alone are holy. All nations will come and worship before You, for Your righteous acts have been revealed (Revelation 15:1-4).*

*Sores on the Wicked* (Revelation 16:2). The result of the emptying of the first bowl of God's wrath will be "ugly and painful sores" on all "who had the mark of the beast and worshiped his image."

*Death of all Marine Life* (Revelation 16:3). When the second angel empties his bowl, the seas will turn red like blood, killing all marine life.

*Drinking Water Contaminated* (Revelation 16:4-7). With the pouring out of the bowl of the third angel, drinking water everywhere will become red like blood. John heard the angel in charge of the waters declare, "You are just in these judgments, You who are and who were, the Holy One, because You have so judged; for they have shed the blood of Your saints and prophets, and You have given them blood to drink as they deserve" (vv. 5,6).

*Scorching Heat* (Revelation 16:8,9). As the fourth angel pours out His bowl of wrath, the heat from the sun will become so intense that it will sear the ungodly. But instead of repenting, they will blaspheme God's name.

*Darkness and Pain* (Revelation 16:10,11). When the fifth angel pours his bowl of wrath upon mankind, the area of earth covered by Antichrist's kingdom will be plunged into darkness. This will intensify the distress brought on by the previous judgments. The people will probably use artificial lighting to carry on. Even though they will know they are experiencing the judgment from God, they will refuse to repent.

*Attack from the East* (Revelation 16:12-16). The pouring of the sixth bowl will cause the Euphrates River to dry up, wiping out the boundary between the Orient and the West. Three evil spirits, depicted as coming out of the mouth of the dragon (the devil), the beast (the Antichrist), and the false prophet (Antichrist's religious cohort), will deceive the leaders of the nations into thinking they can still frustrate God's program by capturing the Middle East. These deluded men will lead their forces—both from the Orient and the West—into the Valley of Megiddo for a final showdown.

*Final Conclusions* (Revelation 16:17-21). When the seventh angel pours out his bowl of wrath into the air, a loud voice will declare, "It is done!" This will be followed by brilliant flashes of lightning that will fill the sky, peals of thunder reverberating throughout the earth, 100-pound hailstones falling from the heavens, and the worst earthquake in all history. The entire globe will shake with such intensity that mountains and islands will disappear. These are like final birth pangs. They will immediately precede the return of the Lord Jesus Christ to destroy His enemies and establish His kingdom. (Read Zechariah 14; Matthew 24:29-31; Revelation 6:12-17; 11:15-19.)

## SUMMARY

We have traced the biblical teaching of the course of the great tribulation, focusing upon its dreadful characteristics. With the opening of the seals, we saw the calamities unsaved people will bring on themselves because they will choose to follow Antichrist. With the sounding of the trumpets, we observed terrible disasters in nature and the frightening results of demonic invasions. We then watched as seven angels poured out their bowls of wrath on the earth—the final series of judgments. One bowl followed the other in rapid succession while the nations were getting ready for one final attempt to frustrate God's purposes. The sixth seal, the seventh trumpet, and the seventh bowl judgment took us to the end of the great tribulation—showing us the dreadful events that will occur as Jesus Christ returns in glory.

In the next four chapters we will fill in a number of significant details we have not yet touched upon. We will consider the great conversion to God that will take place during the tribulation, the fall of the world church, the destruction of Babylon, and the war of Armageddon.

# 6. Salvation During the Great Tribulation

Multiplied thousands of men and women will turn in faith to Jesus Christ and be saved during the second half of Daniel's 70th seven, the great tribulation. I am convinced of this on the basis of both Old and New Testament Scriptures. This 3 and 1/2-year period will unquestionably be the worst time of suffering, devastation, and death in all human history. Yet it will also be one of the best from the eternal perspective, for a vast multitude will believe on Christ. A person who enters the great tribulation, accepts Christ, endures persecution, and then dies will be far better off eternally than one who is born under present circumstances, attains earthly success, enjoys a lifetime of luxury, and then dies unsaved at a ripe old age. We should keep this in mind as we contemplate the terrible things that are going to happen during that brief but awesome period of the outpouring of God's wrath.

## ISRAEL'S SPIRITUAL RENEWAL

The nation of Israel will be converted to Christ during the great tribulation. Of course, this does not mean every individual will be saved, but the majority of Jews living on earth at that time will believe on Jesus. Zechariah 13:8,9 tells us that two-thirds of all Jewish people will be killed in the great tribulation, and that one-third will live through it to enter the kingdom of God. Undoubtedly a large percentage of the Jews who die will be martyred because of their faith in Christ.

Perhaps the most clear and beautiful description of the future spiritual renewal and restoration of Israel is found in Ezekiel 36:16 through chapter 37. Speaking through the prophet, God reminded the Israelites of their sad history, then gave them glowing promises of future blessing. Because of their sinfulness, He poured out His wrath upon them and scattered them throughout the nations. They profaned His holy name wherever they went, thus continuing to make themselves unworthy of His favor. But the Lord has not deserted His people, the Jews. For the sake of His "holy name," He promised that He will one day act on their behalf.

> *For I will take you out of the nations; I will gather you from all the countries and bring you back into your own land. I will sprinkle clean water on you, and you will be clean; I will cleanse you from all your impurities and from all your idols. I will give you a new heart and put a new spirit in you; I will remove from you your heart of stone and give you a heart of flesh. And I will put My Spirit in you and move you to follow My decrees and be careful to keep My laws. You will live in the land I gave your forefathers; you will be My people, and I will be your God (Ezekiel 36:24-28).*

Ezekiel 37 pictures a large number of dry bones coming together, receiving flesh, lying there as dead corpses, and then rising to their feet when God breathes upon them. This portrays the Jewish people gathering in Palestine while still in unbelief, existing as a spiritually dead nation, and then receiving new life through a miracle of God.

# THE TIME OF ISRAEL'S CONVERSION

When will this massive turning to Christ by Israel occur? During the great tribulation! It cannot take place in the church age; neither can it occur during the millennium. All through this age of the church, the Israelites are living in unbelief, as portrayed in Romans 11:25, "I do not want you to be ignorant of this mystery, brothers, so that you may not be conceited: Israel has experienced a hardening in part until the full number of the Gentiles has come in." God will not take away this blindness until after the church age has concluded.

Nor can Israel's conversion occur during the millennium. Why? Because only saved people are allowed to enter God's kingdom, whether on earth or in heaven. Jesus told Nicodemus, "I tell you the truth, unless a man is born again, he cannot see the kingdom of God" (John 3:3). Since the great tribulation will take place between the rapture of the church and the coming of Christ to establish His kingdom, this is the logical time period for Israel's conversion.

# AN ABSOLUTE PREREQUISITE

The conversion of Israel is a precondition for the glorious return of Christ. Jesus will come back as the King and Messiah of the Jews as soon as they (that is, the majority of them) repent and believe on Him. Peter expressed this truth in his second sermon after the Day of Pentecost. Speaking to the Jews, he said:

*Repent, then, and turn to God, so that your sins may be wiped out, that times of refreshing may come from the Lord, and that He may send the Christ, who has been appointed for you—even Jesus. He must remain in heaven until the time comes for God to restore everything, as He promised long ago through His holy prophets (Acts 3:19-21).*

When the majority of the Jewish people accept the Lord Jesus as their Messiah, the great tribulation will come to an end and Christ will make His glorious appearance.

## BORN IN A DAY

Some people who do not take Peter's declaration at face value say that the Jewish people will not believe on Jesus Christ until they see Him coming down from heaven to deliver them from Antichrist. They point to these verses in Zechariah in support of their viewpoint:

*And I will pour out on the house of David and the inhabitants of Jerusalem a spirit of grace and supplication. They will look on Me, the One they have pierced, and mourn for Him as one mourns for an only child, and grieve bitterly for Him as one grieves for a firstborn son. On that day the weeping in Jerusalem will be great, like the weeping of Hadad Rimmon in the plain of Megiddo (Zechariah 12:10,11).*

Yes, these verses declare that the Jews will mourn when they see the Lord Jesus coming down from heaven. But the weeping will be done by those Israelites who already have been converted. They will be so overwhelmed by the tragedy of their long period of unbelief that they will cry with deep remorse and wailing. The sight of Jesus coming to deliver them from the armies of Antichrist will fill them with sadness for their rejection of Him. But their sorrow will soon be turned to joy.

## GENTILE CONVERSIONS

Not only will the majority of Jews be converted during the great tribulation, but great numbers of Gentiles will also turn to Jesus Christ. This fact is clearly depicted in Revelation 7:9-17. In a vision, John saw "a great multitude that no one could count, from every nation, tribe, people and language, standing before the throne and in front of the Lamb" (v. 9). One of the elders identified them as follows:

*These are they who have come out of the great tribulation; they have washed their robes and made them white in the blood of the Lamb. Therefore, they are before the throne of God and serve Him day and night in His temple; and He who sits on the throne will spread His tent over them. Never again will they hunger; never again will they thirst. The sun will not beat upon them, nor any scorching heat. For the Lamb at the center of the throne will be their shepherd; He will lead them to springs of living water. And God will wipe away every tear from their eyes (Revelation 7:14-17).*

This innumerable company, taken from all tribes and nations and families, represents both the Jews and Gentiles. They will believe on Jesus Christ during the great tribulation and will then be martyred for their faith. When they die, their spirits will go to heaven; this is the way they come "out of the great tribulation." Converted Jews and Gentiles who escape the clutches of Antichrist will enter the millennial age in their earthly bodies.

## HOW WILL IT HAPPEN?

Some people say that because all Christians will be removed at the rapture, the likelihood of mass conversions to Christ is slim indeed. They don't see how vast multitudes can be saved if the believers are gone. But I believe the post-rapture setting will be conducive to a turning of people to Christ.

Let's imagine what will take place shortly after the rapture occurs. First, almost everyone will be puzzled, disturbed, frightened, or all three. The sudden disappearance of many people will cause widespread consternation and alarm.

Second, people will be discussing the event everywhere. Some of them will remember that they heard Christians say this kind of thing would happen. People will remark that the ones who are missing are those who talked to them about a personal relationship with Jesus Christ.

Third, many people will likely start reading the Bible and Christian literature, especially books on prophecy. Remember that when we are caught up we will leave our libraries and Bibles behind. They will serve as "preachers" for those who read them.

While all of this is going on, Antichrist and his minister of religion will publish an "explanation" of the event. He will fool some people, but not everyone. Many will accept Christ. The evil world ruler will then demand that he be worshiped as God, and he will turn against all who refuse to do so. At the same time two men, the witnesses of Revelation 11:1-14, will begin to preach Christ and perform miracles. They will be supernaturally protected from harm, and their mighty works will be greater than those performed by Antichrist and his cohorts. In addition, the devastating judgments of God will be falling upon the earth in rapid succession.

In those days no one will question the supernatural! The issue will be clear! People will be confronted with a clear-cut choice. Antichrist will represent everything evil, while the two witnesses will represent everything good. Neutrality will be impossible. God's elected ones, possessing through the Holy Spirit a desire for the truth, will accept Jesus Christ as their Savior. They will take this step even though they know full well that their decision could lead them to their death. In spite of the danger, they will value eternal riches far more than temporary gain in the service of Antichrist.

## OBJECTIONS TO THIS TEACHING

Four primary objections have been raised to the teaching that multitudes will be saved during the great tribulation. Let's look at them in detail.

1. *The Removal of the Restrainer.* I'm not a mind-reader, but I know that you may be thinking that you have caught me in an inconsistency. In a previous chapter, I pointed out that according to 2 Thessalonians 2:7 the Holy Spirit must be "taken out of the way" before Antichrist can be revealed. Now I've been talking about multitudes being saved through the power of the Holy Spirit. How can that take place if He has been removed?

This is not a real difficulty, even though it has been repeated again and again by people who don't accept the pretribulation rapture of the church. The fact is that the Holy Spirit will be very active during the great tribulation. Paul did not say that the Spirit would be removed from the earth, but only that He would be taken "out of the way." One of His functions—that of restrainer—will end with the rapture of the church. His influence through the testimony of God's people will be removed. But in every other way He will continue His ministry on earth.

2. *Strong Delusion.* A second objection to the idea that multitudes will be saved during the great tribulation stems from a misunderstanding of Paul's warning that God will send a powerful delusion upon certain people who are left on earth after the rapture. Some are convinced that this strong delusion will be sent upon everyone who has ever heard the gospel. But to make this claim is to go beyond what Paul said. We read:

*The coming of the lawless one will be in accordance with the work of Satan displayed in all kinds of counterfeit miracles, signs and wonders, and in every sort of evil that deceives those who are perishing. They perish because they refused to love the truth and so be saved. For this reason God sends them a powerful delusion so that they will believe the lie and so that all will be condemned who have not believed the truth but have delighted in wickedness (2 Thessalonians 2:9-12).*

Not everybody who has heard the gospel without responding can be classified as delighting in wickedness. Some hear the story of salvation without understanding it. Some reject it because of the lifestyle they see in people who proclaim it. Given time, and under normal circumstances, many might come to Christ. Paul here is warning people who are deliberately rejecting the truth right now. Some may even ridicule Christians, saying they will believe when they see Jesus come back and not before. We must therefore view these verses as a warning to the presumptuous.

3. *A Second Chance.* Some say that allowing for salvation after the rapture is actually giving people a second chance, which they say is not biblical. What the Bible does deny, however, is a second chance *after*

*death.* How many people accept Jesus Christ the first time they hear the gospel? The vast majority do not! But God graciously comes back again and again with the gospel story. Dear reader, if you are not saved, even though you've heard the gospel many times, do not despair. A poem I memorized years ago offers you hope.

I wish that there were some wonderful place,
Called the Land of Beginning Again,
Where all our mistakes and heartaches,
And all our poor selfish grief,
Could be dropped like a shabby old coat at the door,
And never put on again.

That place is available to you today—at the feet of Jesus. And it will still be there after the rapture. The way to salvation is always open!

But don't delay. Jesus issued a solemn warning, "Walk while you have the light, before darkness overtakes you. . . . Put your trust in the light while you have it" (John 12:35,36). True, "While the candle holds to burn, the vilest sinner may return." The problem isn't a closed door but a heart so calloused that it doesn't want God's salvation. Conscious procrastination is rejection. Don't do it. Every time you say "no" to the call of faith, you cripple your ability to believe, until at last you may be among the number of whom it is written, "they could not believe" (John 12:39).

4. *"They Repented Not."* The fourth objection stems from a number of references in Revelation to people who refused to repent in spite of dire judgment. The survivors of the destruction associated with the sixth trumpet, for example, will not "repent of their murders, their magic arts, their sexual immorality or their thefts" (Revelation 9:21). Nor will people repent when God pours out upon the earth His bowls of wrath. ". . . they refused to repent and glorify Him. . . . but they refused to repent of what they had done. And they cursed God on account of the plague of hail, because the plague was so terrible" (Revelation 16:9,11,21).

These are solemn declarations, but they do not militate against what I said about many people being saved during the great tribulation. These judgments will fall upon the earth as that terrible period draws to a close. By then almost everybody on earth will have made the decision to accept or reject Christ.

## CONCLUSION

Reading about all the terrible things that will happen during the great tribulation can be depressing. It isn't pleasant to contemplate the stark terror, the intense pain, and the overwhelming grief that will mark this brief period of time. It's mind-boggling to think about more than half of the earth's population (perhaps about two-thirds) being killed during this brief span of 3 and 1/2 years. But the picture is brightened considerably when we think about the tremendous company of people who will be saved. Heaven will be greatly enriched by the presence of that innumerable host of Jewish and Gentile believers who will be taken out of the great tribulation by dying as martyrs.

I believe millions of people in heaven will testify that the awesome events associated with the rapture and the great tribulation were the means of their salvation. They may say something like this: "I was careless and indifferent during the church age. I paid little attention to people who tried to tell me about Jesus Christ and salvation. But when the rapture occurred, I began to think seriously about these matters. Then, when the evil world ruler I had admired began his program of dreadful persecution against the Jewish people, I saw that the Bible prophecies were true. In the midst of frightening, death-dealing catastrophes, I placed my trust in Jesus Christ. I was soon arrested, tortured, and then executed. But here I am, a trophy of God's grace. The great tribulation was an awful time, but it was a wonderful time for me because it brought about my salvation."

How much better it would be to receive Christ now!

# 7. The Destruction of Ecclesiastical Babylon

Building a worldwide, unified religious system is the goal of the ecumenicists today. It will enjoy a brief period of success during the tribulation period—only to meet with a disastrous end. The religious leaders who are trying to bring under one banner people of every belief—Muslim, Buddhist, Hindu, spiritualist, the cults, and liberal Christendom—represent an ancient pagan system that may correctly be called "Babylonianism."

Representatives of this system of world religion will always be active and will become extremely strong in the endtime. Babylonianism is portrayed in its final form in Revelation 17 under the symbolism of a gorgeously attired harlot on whose forehead are inscribed the words: MYSTERY BABYLON THE GREAT THE MOTHER OF PROSTITUTES AND OF THE ABOMINATIONS OF THE EARTH (v. 5). In this chapter we will trace the story of Babylonianism from beginning to end.

# NIMROD, THE MIGHTY HUNTER

Ancient legends tell of a man named Nimrod Bar-Cush as the founder of a religious system that dominated the Middle East for centuries. The Bible doesn't specifically identify him with this pagan religion, but it does tell us that he founded cities which later became prominent centers in the Assyrian and Babylonian empires.

> *Cush was the father of Nimrod, who grew to be a mighty warrior on the earth. He was a mighty hunter before the Lord; that is why it is said, "Like Nimrod, a mighty hunter before the Lord." The first centers of his kingdom were Babylon, Erech, Akkad and Calneh, in Shinar. From that land he went to Assyria, where he built Nineveh, Rehoboth Ir, Calah and Resen, which is between Nineveh and Calah; that is the great city (Genesis 10:8-12).*

The declaration that Nimrod was "a mighty hunter before the Lord" probably refers to him hunting down men to subjugate them. Dr. Harold J. Stigers, after analyzing the biblical data in the light of information found in other documents, concluded, "Thus he established a thoroughly autocratic, imperialistic, despotic system of tyrannical government (of a kind described in Isaiah, chapters 13 and 14), back of which stands Satan in all his rage against God" (*A Commentary on Genesis,* Zondervan, 1976, p. 125). It was in this Nimrod-founded culture that the religious system called Babylonianism was born and developed.

The nonbiblical ancient documents that mention Nimrod vary in many details, and they often mix myth and legend with history. Therefore, we cannot draw a completely accurate picture of this man or his life. According to some accounts he married a woman named Semiramus, who became the first high priestess of the Babylonian religious system. Legends tell of her giving birth to a miraculously conceived son who was named Tammuz. In the Babylonian Saga he was seduced by Ishtar, the goddess of fertility. When she betrayed him, he died, descended to the underworld, came back to the earth of mankind, and then returned to the nether regions. Thus he was the deity who came to symbolize the dying and rising of vegetation as it occurs with the rotating of the seasons. Apparently this led to the development of pagan fertility rites involving male and female deities, temple prostitutes, and sexual orgies. This was the beginning of Babylonianism.

## THE TOWER OF BABEL

When, after mentioning Nimrod, Moses went on to record the Tower of Babel incident, he gave us a clear picture of ancient Babylonianism. The people who tried to erect this tower did so in revolt against God. They were definitely resisting His command to scatter over the earth, and they sought to keep the people in one location by establishing a pagan worship center. This is the reason the Lord was so displeased with their attempt. We read:

*Now the whole world had one language and a common speech. As men moved eastward, they found a plain in Shinar and settled there.*

*They said to each other, "Come, let's make bricks and bake them thoroughly." They used brick instead of stone, and tar instead of mortar. Then they said, "Come, let us build ourselves a city, with a tower that reaches to the heavens, so that we may make a name for ourselves and not be scattered over the face of the whole earth."*

*But the Lord came down to see the city and the tower that the men were building. The Lord said, "If as one people speaking the same language they have begun to do this, then nothing they plan to do will be impossible for them. Come, let Us go down and confuse their language so they will not understand each other."*

*So the Lord scattered them from there over all the earth, and they stopped building the city. That is why it was called Babel—because there the Lord confused the language of the whole world. From there the Lord scattered them over the face of the whole earth (Genesis 11:1-9).*

That this tower was intended to be a pagan worship

center is indicated by two factors: (a) God's reaction to this project, and (b) the testimony of archeology. Many ziggurats have been uncovered, and they all contain drawings that tell us they were dedicated to the worship of the heavenly bodies and pagan gods. They also reveal to us that man had developed a complex astrology long before the time of Abraham. Interestingly, this attempt to build a tower was made in the plain of Shinar, a place near the ancient city of Babylon. It was an act of rebellion against God, it involved a scheme for unification, and it featured a highly developed astrology.

## WORLDWIDE DISPERSION

The religious system built upon the story of Tammuz spread rapidly throughout the ancient world. The names of the gods and goddesses were different in each country, and so were some of the details of the stories. But the worship of Baal in Canaan, of Dagon in Philistia, of Moloch in Phoenicia, of Ra, Horus, Set, and Bar in Egypt, and the hierarchy of gods and goddesses in Greece and Rome possessed many similarities. The varieties in the names and stories are not important. It is significant, however, that all of them featured the same dedication of virgins to religious prostitution, the same sprinkling of holy water, the same legends about a mother (the queen of heaven) who gave birth to a supernaturally conceived child, and the same myths about this son dying and returning. These legends and myths continued to be taught in Greece and Rome long after the intellectual leaders of these countries had lost faith in them. They were retained simply because they exerted a unifying force within their nations.

## INFILTRATION

Satan, the founder and developer of this false religious system, knew that the best way to hinder God's people was through infiltration. He realized that an all-out, open attack wouldn't work, and he knew that he was no match for God. Therefore his plan was to introduce elements of paganism into Israel. He accomplished this by leading the Israelites to fraternize with their pagan neighbors.

The devil was remarkably successful. He was able to draw the people of Israel into many of the practices of their heathen neighbors. In the wilderness they made and worshiped a golden calf, a copy of the bull that served as a symbol of Canaan. Later, they repeatedly became involved in the worship of the pagan Canaanite deities, Baal and Asherah. During the rules of Saul, David, and Solomon, the Israelites were quite separated from idolatry. But after Solomon's death, they went right back into it.

In spite of periodic revivals in Judah, the Jews became more and more involved in elements of this Babylonian system. The 10 northern tribes were taken into captivity by Assyria. But even then the two tribes—the southern kingdom—didn't learn. A few years before God let Judah be conquered by Babylon, He told Jeremiah, "The children gather wood, the fathers light the fire, and the women knead the dough and make cakes of bread for the Queen of Heaven" (Jeremiah 7:18). On another occasion the citizens of Judah, though on the brink of national disaster, defiantly addressed God's faithful prophet as follows:

*We will not listen to the message you have spoken to us in the name of the Lord! We will certainly do everything we said we would: We will burn incense to the Queen of Heaven and will pour out drink offerings to her just as we and our fathers, our kings and our officials did in the towns of Judah and in the streets of Jerusalem. At that time we had plenty of food and were well off and suffered no harm. But ever since we stopped burning incense to the Queen of Heaven and pouring out drink offerings to her, we have had nothing and have been perishing by sword and famine (Jeremiah 44:16-18).*

It appears that the people in Judah responded for a brief time to Jeremiah's preaching and discontinued their sacrifices to this Babylonian female deity. But they did so reluctantly, and as a result they did not experience God's blessing. Now they were using their unfavorable conditions as an excuse for going back to Babylonianism.

The prophet Ezekiel, while ministering to Jews who had already been taken into captivity by Babylon, was given a series of visions in which he saw the idolatrous abominations going on in Jerusalem. Transported in spirit to this special city, he saw God's people worshiping an image (8:1-6), beheld them participating in secret, mysterious animal cult rites (8:7-13), watched women weeping for Tammuz (8:14,15), and observed 25 men bowing before the sun (8:16). All of these abominations were directly or indirectly drawn from ancient Babylonianism. The unbelieving among the Israelites were easily drawn into this pagan system in its various forms.

The period of captivity cured the Israelites of their fascination with idolatry. When they entered territories where the people were wholly devoted to paganism, they were revolted by what they saw. They founded synagogues and returned, at least outwardly, to the worship of Jehovah.

## FROM PAUL TO CONSTANTINE

The Babylonian religious system played a prominent role in the persecution of Christians during the second and third centuries after Christ. The devil, the mastermind behind all false religion, apparently thought he could destroy the church through persecution. He first opposed Christians through Judaism, and then he used the Roman state. Behind the governing authorities in Rome were the priests of the pagan mystery religions.

The most intense persecution of believers was caused by their refusal to ascribe the title "lord" to the Roman emperor. This demand originated with the pagan priests. They initiated each emperor into the mysteries of their faith, declared him to be a god, and urged him to insist upon being called "lord." When the Christians resisted, declaring that Jesus Christ alone is Lord, they were imprisoned, tortured, and executed. Thousands upon thousands died as martyrs—but the church flourished. Satan could not achieve his objective through open opposition.

## CONSTANTINE TO THE PRESENT TIME

The devil changed his tactics after A.D. 300, when the Roman emperor Constantine became a "convert" to the Christian faith. From this point on, Satan succeeded in bringing about an amalgamation of Babylonianism and Christianity.

Constantine's lifestyle didn't change very much after his professed conversion to Christ. He ordered the execution of his wife Fausta and his son Crispus. He dedicated his new capital with a half-Christian, half-pagan ceremony. He may have turned to Christianity because he saw it as a means of restoring unity to his empire. He and his successors were not able to bring about the complete merger of Babylonianism and Christianity, but they did manage to introduce many pagan beliefs and practices into Christendom.

First, an early bishop of Rome "christianized" a pagan phrase, "the keeper of the bridge." In the false religions the "bridge" was the connecting link between a worshiper and Satan. This Roman bishop had the emblem of a fish head and the words "the keeper of the bridge" engraved on his ring. This ring was passed on to each successor.

Second, the title *pontifex maximus,* which had belonged exclusively to the Roman emperors after they were initiated into the mystery religion, was conferred upon the bishops of Rome.

Third, the virgin mother, called the Queen of Heaven, and her child, so prominent in the Babylonian system, began to be depicted in churches everywhere as objects of veneration.

Fourth, the sprinkling of holy water began to take on great significance in church doctrine. This rite figured largely in the cleansing rituals of paganism, but it is not even mentioned, much less advocated, in the New Testament.

Fifth, the leaders in Christendom began to make a wide distinction between the clergy and the laity. The ascription of special power to a favored few went hand-in-hand with the growth of sacramentalism, which claimed that certain rituals and ordinances had saving and life-changing value. All of this was drawn from the mystery religions, not from the New Testament or apostolic example.

Sixth, the church became increasingly identified with the state. Tied closely to the government, it became wealthy and worldly. Every baby born as a citizen of the land was automatically a church member. Government leaders levied taxes for the church in exchange for the backing of priests and bishops. Christendom gradually became a monstrous ecclesiastical-political system with little true spiritual authority.

Not all Christians, of course, became members of the Roman Catholic or Eastern Orthodox churches, even during the Middle Ages. Believers who held to the doctrine of separation of church and state continued to meet in small groups. The Reformation came as a much-needed corrective, and it made a great impact upon many who had grown up as Roman Catholics. Even so, the state-church concept was not universally abandoned. To this very day, Catholic, Orthodox, and some Protestant denominations are being subsidized by the government in certain countries.

The current ecumenical movement is the modern form of Babylonianism. Its leaders, most of whom take an active role in the World Council of Churches, have little regard for the historic doctrines of the Christian faith. They advocate the uniting of all the world's religions—Buddhist, Muslim, Hindu, and Christian sects, including spiritists—into one super-church. While affirming the doctrine of separation of church and state, they try to exert a strong influence upon government. And they usually side with liberal, God-denying, Christ-rejecting groups.

## FROM RAPTURE TO RETURN

After the church is taken out by the rapture, Babylonianism will flourish for a time, then it will be thoroughly dismantled. Revelation 17 explains the final rise and fall of this religious system, portraying it as a gorgeously attired harlot who will work hand-in-glove with the government of Antichrist. We read:

> One of the seven angels who had the seven bowls came and said to me, "Come, I will show you the punishment of the great prostitute, who sits on many waters. With her the kings of the earth committed adultery and the inhabitants of the earth were intoxicated with the wine of her adulteries."
>
> Then the angel carried me away in the Spirit into a desert. There I saw a woman sitting on a scarlet beast that was covered with blasphemous names and had seven heads and ten horns. The woman was dressed in purple and scarlet, and was glittering with gold, precious stones, and pearls. She held a golden cup in her hand, filled with abominable things and the filth of her adulteries. This title was written on her forehead:
>
> MYSTERY
> BABYLON THE GREAT
> THE MOTHER OF PROSTITUTES
> AND OF THE ABOMINATIONS
> OF THE EARTH.
>
> I saw that the woman was drunk with the blood of the saints, the blood of those who bore testimony to Jesus (Revelation 17:1-6).

The seven-headed beast with 10 horns represents Antichrist and his kingdom. The seven heads, also referred to as seven mountains and seven kings, could be an oblique reference to the city of Rome. But the term "mountain" is a synonym for "kingdom" in many Old Testament passages. In Jeremiah 51:25, for example, God calls Babylon a destroying *mountain* that destroys all the earth.

The seven heads therefore primarily symbolize seven world powers, five of which had already fallen by the time of John's writing. They are Egypt, Assyria,

Babylon, Medo-Persia, and Greece. The sixth one is undoubtedly Rome, the empire in power when John recorded his vision. The seventh empire, of whose ruler we read, ". . . the other has not yet come; and when he does come, he must remain for a little while" (Revelation 17:10), refers either to Diocletian's quadripartite or to an endtime confederacy of nations that will be taken over by Antichrist when he gains world rule. He will be the eighth world ruler.

The beast also is pictured as having 10 horns. Their significance is stated as follows:

*The ten horns you saw are ten kings who have not yet received a kingdom, but who for one hour will receive authority as kings along with the beast (Revelation 17:12).*

This explanation is in perfect harmony with the picture of the coming world dictator and his kingdom that is portrayed in Daniel 2 and 7. The horns represent 10 nations that will constitute the empire of this coming world ruler.

The harlot of Revelation 17 symbolizes the religious system that will be sponsored by the ecumenicists of the endtime. The harlot and the beast will cooperate for a time. She will actively assist Antichrist and the false prophet when they inaugurate the dreadful persecution against believers, described in Revelation 13. This is the meaning of Revelation 17:6, which portrays her as "drunk with the blood of the saints, the blood of those who bore testimony to Jesus."

This period of cooperation will not last long, however. After Antichrist and the false prophet have securely established their position, they will enlist the help of 10 government leaders within their kingdom to destroy this mongrelized form of Christendom. We read:

*The beast and the ten horns you saw will hate the prostitute. They will bring her to ruin and leave her naked; they will eat her flesh and burn her with fire. For God has put it into their hearts to accomplish His purpose by agreeing to give the beast their power to rule,*

*until God's words are fulfilled. The woman you saw
is the great city that rules over the kings of the earth
(Revelation 17:16-18).*

As John finished his description of the destruction of
the harlot, he referred to her as "the great city that
rules over the kings of the earth" (v. 18). This may
seem to contradict what we said about her symbolizing
the final form of ecumenicism. But you will notice that
this is Babylon in its *mystery form,* not the city itself.
This mystery form is the religious system that
originated in Babylon and has exerted such
tremendous political power down through the ages.

This "destruction" will not necessarily involve the
bombing or shelling of any city or buildings. (The
expressions "leave her naked," "eat her flesh," and
"burn her with fire" in verse 16 are to be taken
symbolically, because the harlot to whom they refer is
a symbol.) We know, for example, that the Roman
Catholic and Mormon churches could be "destroyed"
without the Vatican or Salt Lake City being
demolished. A dictatorial government would only need
to arrest, imprison, and perhaps execute their leaders
and confiscate their property. This is undoubtedly
what Antichrist and the false prophet will do at some
point during the 3 and 1/2-year period before Christ's
glorious return.

# 8. The Destruction of Commercial Babylon

In the preceding chapter we discussed Babylonianism, the religious system portrayed symbolically in Revelation 17 as a gorgeously attired harlot riding on a monstrous beast. After identifying her, we traced her history, depicted her moment of triumph, and observed her sudden end. We pointed out that the religionists who were left behind at the rapture will organize a new world church. It will be made up of people from every conceivable religious background, including those involved in the occult. This powerful organization symbolized by the harlot will be backed by the government of Antichrist, the endtime world dictator depicted by the beast with seven heads and ten horns. As soon as this wicked ruler feels secure, he and his cohorts will destroy the world church, probably by executing her leaders and confiscating her property.

Revelation 18 also speaks of Babylon, but the picture is completely different from that of Revelation 17.

Chapter 18 opens with an angel announcing the impending destruction of a mighty city (vv. 1-3). Then "another voice from heaven" (v. 4) calls upon God's people to leave before judgment falls. After the great city is demolished, political leaders, merchants, and maritime personnel will weep (vv. 9-19). They will grieve over the financial losses caused by the city's collapse. The chapter closes by taking us back to the time just before the city's destruction. It portrays a mighty angel as he picks up a huge boulder, casts it into the sea, and delivers an ode against the city (vv. 21-24).

The study of Revelation 18 gives rise to many questions. Is this passage describing the ancient city of Babylon? Or is it speaking of Rome? New York? Tokyo? In this chapter we will survey the biblical evidence to see if we can identify the great city that is fallen and determine when this prophecy will be fulfilled.

## IDENTITY OF BABYLON

When we try to identify the Babylon depicted in Revelation 18, we come up with four reasonable possibilities: (1) Rome; (2) an unnamed city in Europe, Asia, or America; (3) the United States; or (4) ancient Babylon rebuilt on its old site. We will consider each alternative in detail.

*Rome.* Most biblical expositors consider Rome to be the Babylon of Revelation 18. This city was the capital of the Roman Empire. It has long been the seat of the Roman Catholic Church, the ecclesiastical body that adopted so many of the beliefs and practices of the Babylonian mystery religions. Furthermore, the fact that the seven heads on the beast represent not only seven kings but also "seven mountains" (17:9) may point to Rome, "the city of seven hills." These mountains may also refer to seven successive kingdoms of the Roman Empire. Furthermore, it seems logical that after Antichrist assassinates the leaders of the world church and confiscates her property, he may make this city the capital of his kingdom.

The interpretation of the term "Babylon" as a reference to the city of Rome is supported by the most common interpretation of 1 Peter 5:13, "She who is in Babylon, chosen together with you, sends you her greetings . . . ." Most Bible scholars, past and present, believe that Peter wrote this epistle while in Rome. Whether the greeting came from Peter's wife (the generally accepted Greek text has only the feminine definite article), or from the church as the "elect lady" (2 John 1), has no real bearing on this problem. As far as we know, all church leaders before the Reformation understood Peter to be making a reference to Rome. They said that he used the term "Babylon" to describe Rome because it had become the very center of organized godlessness. Ancient Babylon therefore eloquently depicted the moral and spiritual degeneration of the community where these saints resided.

These are good reasons for adopting the view that the Babylon of Revelation 18 is Rome. It could very well serve as the seat of the apostate world church of the great tribulation period and as the capital of Antichrist's empire. Erich Sauer points out some interesting facts about this city. It began about 1,000 B.C. as a poor village, grew to a city of one million by A.D. 100, was reduced to a small town of less than 50,000 inhabitants after the barbaric invasions, and today is once again a great city with several million inhabitants. Beyond any question, Rome has been the center of religious Babylonianism for many centuries. How fitting it is that this ancient city should become the capital of Antichrist's kingdom!

*An Unnamed City in Europe, Asia, Africa, or America.* A number of Bible students believe that we don't have enough evidence to identify the Babylon portrayed in Revelation 18. They think it best to be indefinite, concluding only that it will be a large city somewhere on our planet.

*The United States of America.* In recent years a few Bible students have suggested that the United States is the commercial Babylon of Revelation 18, pointing out that it has become the world's leader in industry, commerce, and finance. I think this idea has little merit, however. Why would John use the term "city" if he were thinking of a nation? Moreover, why should the United States be singled out for special punishment? We are by no means the most immoral country in the world. And we have sent out more missionaries than any other land. I suppose the Babylon of Revelation 18 could be a great city in the United States, but it is not the entire country. It could just as well be a large city in some other part of the world.

*Babylon on the Euphrates.* The fourth possibility is that the city referred to in Revelation 18 is ancient Babylon, which would be rebuilt at or near its original site. The Bible students who have taken this position are convinced that a literal fulfillment of prophecy demands this viewpoint. They point out that according to Isaiah 13:9, Babylon will be destroyed during the "day of the Lord," a term which usually denotes the great tribulation period yet to come. The prophet went on to declare that the city will be demolished suddenly and completely. So thorough will be the destruction that the area will become uninhabited except for jackals, hyenas, wild goats, and owls.

A reading of Jeremiah 51 gives the same impression. In this chapter, God declares that Babylon will be "desolate forever." He went on to say that she would "sink to rise no more because of the disaster I will bring upon her" (v. 64).

The actual history of Babylon doesn't seem to match the descriptions given in these two chapters. The Medes and Persians had a relatively easy time when they captured her. They didn't tear down her walls or burn her buildings. Herodotus said that they diverted the Euphrates River and marched into the city through the dried-up riverbed. Other historians have uncovered evidence that traitors opened the gates for the Persian armies. In any case, they did not destroy the city. Neither did Greece under Alexander the Great. Nor did the Roman forces. Ancient Babylon simply deteriorated through neglect. It gradually became unimportant to world leaders. But it continued to stand. In fact, Babylon wasn't completely abandoned until shortly after A.D. 100. Because a small city called Hilla stands near its ruins today, one may conclude that the complete desolation predicted in Isaiah 13 and Jeremiah 51 has not occurred.

Now, some Bible students are convinced that the prophecies about Babylon are fulfilled by the gradual decline of the city and its generally barren condition today. They see no prophetic need for the city to be rebuilt, to flourish, and to be devastated again. But many good Bible scholars are convinced otherwise. They believe that to fulfill the prophetic Scriptures, the city must be rebuilt, become the capital of Antichrist's kingdom, and then be destroyed.

One problem they face is that the time between the rapture of the church and Christ's return in glory is too brief for the rebuilding of the city. I believe, however, that with modern technology a great city could be built in 2 or 3 years. Besides, the rebuilding process could begin before the rapture occurs. For the past 10 years or so, rumors have persisted that the government of Iraq is planning to build a great city on the site of ancient Babylon. There has even been the mention of constructing a reproduction of the tower of Babel as a tourist attraction. As far as I know, construction has not yet begun. But things sometimes do change very quickly!

A few Bible scholars have presented the idea that Babylon on the Euphrates will be rebuilt and destroyed, but that it will be a small city—not like the Babylon of Revelation 18. They recognize the difficulty of building the city from scratch and making it a world trade center within the span of less than 2 years. Yet they are convinced that the prophecies of Isaiah 13 and Jeremiah 51 have not been literally fulfilled. Therefore, they suggest that a small city will be built on the Euphrates, and that it will serve as the headquarters for Antichrist's religious system after he and his cohorts have destroyed the world church. They believe that the prophecy about the woman and the basket in Zechariah 5:5-11 supports this view.

In summary, I do not believe we can dogmatically identify the Babylon of Revelation 18. That disclosure will not be made until the prophecy is in the process of fulfillment. I have set forth the most likely possibilities, but I feel that nothing is to be gained by insisting upon one theory and denying the validity of the others.

## REASONS FOR DESTRUCTION

The Lord told us that He will destroy commercial Babylon. Its citizens will be sinful, cruel, arrogant, and actively anti-God. We read:

*Then I heard another voice from heaven say: "Come out of her, My people, so that you will not share in her sins, so that you will not receive any of her plagues; for her sins are piled up to heaven, and God has remembered her crimes. Give back to her as she has given; pay her back double for what she has done. Mix her a double portion from her own cup. Give her as much torture and grief as the glory and luxury she gave herself. In her heart she boasts, 'I sit as queen; I am not a widow, and I will never mourn.' Therefore in one day her plagues will overtake her: death, mourning and famine. She will be consumed by fire, for mighty is the Lord God who judges her."*

*"The light of a lamp will never shine in you again. The voice of bridegroom and bride will never be heard in you again. Your merchants were the world's great men. By your magic spell all the nations were led astray. In her was found the blood of prophets and of the saints, and of all who have been killed on the earth"* (Revelation 18:4-8,23,24).

Commercial Babylon—whether Rome, some other great city, or Babylon on the Euphrates—will be the capital of Antichrist's empire. It will also become the center of his religious system. He and his false prophet will demand emperor worship, defy God, and persecute the Lord's people. His followers will be proud, self-sufficient, superstitious, and bitterly opposed to the truth. But God will punish them, making them an example to the rest of mankind, warning them that His terrible wrath will fall upon the earth.

## THE TIME OF BABYLON'S DESTRUCTION

The apostle John doesn't tell us exactly where the destruction of commercial Babylon fits into the chronology of the great tribulation, but we can identify the time with some degree of confidence. We know it will occur after the destruction of religious Babylon, the world church—depicted as a harlot in Revelation 17. It probably will take place while Antichrist is feverishly engaged in the war of Armageddon, therefore occurring a few days or weeks before the end of the great tribulation. We can be quite certain about this because the destruction of Babylon is part of the seventh bowl judgment. We read:

> *The seventh angel poured out his bowl into the air, and out of the temple came a loud voice from the throne, saying, "It is done!" Then there came flashes of lightning, rumblings, peals of thunder and a severe earthquake. No earthquake like it has ever occurred since man has been on earth, so tremendous was the quake. The great city split into three parts, and the cities of the nations collapsed. God remembered Babylon the Great and gave her the cup filled with the wine of the fury of His wrath. Every island fled away and the mountains could not be found. From the sky huge hailstones of about a hundred pounds each fell upon men. And they cursed God on account of the plague of hail, because the plague was so terrible (Revelation 16:17-21).*

True, political leaders and merchants will weep over their financial losses when commercial Babylon falls. But that doesn't imply that the city will be destroyed by natural means. Wicked people have the capacity to become immune to disasters that kill others as long as they themselves are in a place of relative safety. During savage wars, many have made huge profits by selling war equipment, getting rich on products that kill and maim. Therefore, I believe commercial Babylon will be supernaturally destroyed just before Antichrist and his armies are defeated by Christ at Armageddon.

To review, commercial Babylon will be a large city somewhere in the world. It will become the capital of Antichrist's kingdom. It will be filled with arrogant, self-sufficient, cruel, and God-hating citizens. And just before the Lord Jesus comes back to begin His glorious reign, He will wipe that proud city off the face of the earth.

# 9. The War of Armageddon

When I was a child, I felt a sense of awe that bordered on fear whenever I heard someone speak about "Armageddon." This was because I equated it with the end of the world. I visualized the dead from all the ages being raised from their graves to stand at the great white throne for judgment. I thought of myself as being among them. I also had a mental image of great destruction, of our planet burning up, and of the new heavens and new earth replacing it. I found the whole concept somewhat scary, but I also derived comfort from it. I was confident that God and righteousness would ultimately triumph over Satan and evil.

I still believe in a final resurrection, the great white throne judgment, the eventual dissolving of our earth-system, and the emergence of the new heavens and new earth. But I no longer associate these occurrences with the name "Armageddon." I am now convinced that the battle of Armageddon will be the final clash of a war that will be waged toward the close of the great tribulation period.

In this chapter we will trace the war of Armageddon from beginning to end. We will do so by bringing together the key Scripture passages that refer to it, using these biblical references to develop a chronological sequence of events. In so doing, however, I will be quite cautious. The prophecies associated with our Lord's first coming became clear as they were fulfilled, and the same will be true with the endtime prophetic declarations about Armageddon. But Bible prophecy is not simply prewritten history. God apparently doesn't want us to know every detail in advance, so we must use caution about some things as we set forth what we believe the Scriptures tell us.

## PRELUDE TO THE WAR

After the beast, the Western ruler whom we have identified as Antichrist, has exercised absolute power over all mankind for about 3 years, he will begin to encounter some organized resistance. A group of powerful nations will challenge his control of Palestine. Remember, Antichrist will pose as Israel's friend for a time, but he will suddenly show his true colors as her enemy. I believe that the destruction of Russia and her allies, as described in Ezekiel 38 and 39, is the event that will trigger this change. With the northern confederacy out of the way, the wicked Western ruler will seize the rebuilt temple in Jerusalem, demand that he be worshiped, and initiate a time of horrible persecution against all who refuse to comply. Millions of Jews and Gentiles will turn to Christ and suffer martyrdom. God will allow Antichrist only 42 months of rule (Revelation 13:5). As that allotted timespan draws to its close, the Lord will stir up organized resistance around the world. He will use evil spirits to induce the leaders of nations to prepare for a campaign to wrest the control of Palestine from the beast. We read:

*The sixth angel poured out his bowl on the great river Euphrates, and its water was dried up to prepare the way for the kings from the East. Then I saw three evil spirits that looked like frogs; they came out of the mouth of the dragon, out of the mouth of the beast and out of the mouth of the false prophet. They are spirits of demons performing miraculous signs, and they go out to the kings of the whole world, to gather them for the battle on the great day of God Almighty.*

*"Behold, I come like a thief! Blessed is he who stays awake and keeps his clothes with him, so that he may not go naked and be shamefully exposed."*

*Then they gathered the kings together to the place that in Hebrew is called Armageddon (Revelation 16:12-16).*

This confederacy of nations probably will be made up of countries east of Palestine. The Euphrates River, which divides them from the Palestinian region, will be dried up. These national leaders will make plans to gather their armies at "the hill of Megiddo" (the literal meaning of Armageddon), which is located on the southern rim of the plain of Esdraelon. They will decide upon this place to launch an attack against Antichrist's army.

## A BRIEF DIGRESSION

Let me pause here to discuss what I consider to be a common mistake—the idea that the "kings from the East" mentioned in Revelation 16:12 will lead 200 million soldiers to Palestine. This figure is drawn from a misinterpretation of Revelation 9:13-21, which tells of 200 million "mounted troops." Their horses have heads like lions, belch fire, smoke, and sulpher from their mouths, and sting people with their tails. Their riders wear red, dark blue, and yellow breastplates.

These horses and riders are not human soldiers, but are prophetic symbols of demons. Remember, Bible scholars are in almost universal agreement that the locusts with the power to sting like scorpions described in Revelation 9:1-11 are evil spirits. No good reason can be given for changing the symbolism of Revelation 9:13-21. Besides, consistency in Bible interpretation demands that the monstrosities depicted in these verses also represent evil spirits.

I believe the armies that mobilize in the East will be well under 200 million in number. One reason is that this event will occur quite late in the great tribulation, after a large percentage of mankind has already been killed. Even so, the force will be large enough to alarm Antichrist and lead him to prepare for a major conflict.

## THE BEGINNING OF THE WAR

The war of Armageddon will begin when the forces of Antichrist engage the armies of "the king of the South" and "the king of the North." (This will occur before the arrival of the troops from the East and the North.) We read about this confrontation in Daniel.

*At the time of the end the king of the South will engage him in battle, and the king of the North will storm out against him with chariots and cavalry and a great fleet of ships. He will invade many countries and sweep through them like a flood. He will also invade the Beautiful Land. Many countries will fall, but Edom, Moab and the leaders of Ammon will be delivered from his hand. He will extend his power over many countries; Egypt will not escape. He will gain control of the treasures of gold and silver and all the riches of Egypt, with the Libyans and Nubians in submission (Daniel 11:40-43).*

The "king of the South" is the leader of a confederacy of nations located south of Israel, and the "king of the North" is the head of a confederacy of nations north of Palestine. Apparently they will be emboldened by the news of the impending invasion from the East and decide to strike. Keep in mind our conclusion that Russia and her allies will no longer be in the picture as major powers, for they will have been destroyed supernaturally some 3 years or so before the beginning of the war of Armageddon (see Ezekiel 38,39).

The forces of the kings of the South and North (not the far north of Ezekiel 38 and 39) will be soundly defeated by the beast's armies. It appears that Antichrist will flood Palestine with troops to reinforce his standing army. He will march through every country in the Middle East except those small areas once occupied by the Edomites, Moabites, and Ammonites. He will reaffirm his authority in Palestine, quell pockets of resistance, and kill thousands of people.

While Antichrist is engaged in reestablishing his authority in the Middle East, he will hear the disturbing news that armies from the Orient are approaching Palestine. In violent anger, and with a fierce determination to destroy these foes, he will march his troops rapidly into the Jerusalem area and set up quarters in the vicinity of Mt. Zion. Daniel wrote:

> *But reports from the east and the north will alarm him, and he will set out in a great rage to destroy and annihilate many. He will pitch his royal tents between the seas at the beautiful holy mountain. Yet he will come to his end, and no one will help him (Daniel 11:44,45).*

The scenario I have set forth places all the events predicted in Daniel 11:40-45 during the last few months of the great tribulation. Many excellent Bible teachers don't agree, but instead see these occurrences as taking place over a period of at least 3 and 1/2 years. They view the conflict between Antichrist and his first enemies—the king of the South and the king of the North—as a midpoint event of Antichrist's 7-year covenant with the Jews. They interpret the attack by the king of the North as being the attempted invasion of Palestine by Russia and her allies as described in Ezekiel 38 and 39. Antichrist's march through the "glorious land," they feel, will occur when he takes control of Palestine at the beginning of his brief rule. Having put down all opposition, he will establish his Middle East military headquarters on the slopes of Mt. Zion, little realizing that he is only 3 and 1/2 years from destruction.

This latter interpretation of Daniel 11:40-45 seems to make good sense, but in my opinion it presents at least two problems. First, it doesn't fit the context. Second, it gives the forces of Antichrist a greater hand in the defeat of Russia than Ezekiel does.

The first difficulty stems from the context, which portrays Antichrist as having achieved his position of absolute authority. But this situation is highly unlikely until after Russia and her confederates are out of the way. In fact, the defeat of these Northern Powers, as described in Ezekiel 38 and 39, will probably clear the way for Antichrist's takeover as world leader. Notice in Daniel's prophecy how firmly entrenched he seems to be:

*The king will do as he pleases. He will exalt and magnify himself above every god and will say unheard-of things against the God of gods. He will be successful until the time of wrath is completed, for what has been determined must take place. He will show no regard for the gods of his fathers or for the one desired by women, nor will he regard any god, but will exalt himself above them all. Instead of them, he will honor a god of fortresses; a god unknown to his fathers he will honor with gold and silver, with precious stones and costly gifts. He will attack the mightiest fortresses with the help of a foreign god and will greatly honor those who acknowledge him. He will make them rulers over many people and will distribute the land at a price (Daniel 11:36-39).*

A second problem with the view that the Russian invasion is part of the war of Armageddon is the way the armies of this Northern Confederation are defeated. According to Ezekiel 38 and 39, Russia and her allies will not be defeated by Antichrist and his forces but by judgments that God sends from heaven. Through these supernatural events the Lord will destroy many of the troops. The survivors will be thrown into such a panic that they will slay one another. Ezekiel doesn't give human armies much of a role in the defeat of this army, but Daniel says nothing about supernatural judgments. The prophets seem to be describing two completely different battles.

In summary, I believe the battle with the king of the North and South depicted in Daniel 11:40-45 will occur just a few months before Christ returns in glory. But

I express this viewpoint with the realization that the details of this prophecy will not be crystal-clear until they are in the process of actual fulfillment. We are all in for some surprises!

## THE BATTLE OF ARMAGEDDON

The final stage of the war of Armageddon will take place when the armies from the Orient arrive in Palestine. The leaders of these troops will oppose the beast, but they will share his intense hatred for God and the Jewish people. They and their followers will have lived through a major part of the great tribulation without repenting and turning to God. They will be just as determined as Antichrist to destroy every Jew and Gentile who worships the Lord. If they were forced to choose between the rule of Christ or Antichrist, they would prefer the latter. They won't want the beast to have absolute control of the Middle East, but they will join forces with him when they see Jesus Christ come down from heaven.

When the battle of Armageddon begins, the invading forces will immediately capture sections of Jerusalem. The Jewish inhabitants of Jerusalem who are caught in the middle of all this conflict will suffer greatly. Some will flee. Others will be taken as prisoners. Here is what Zechariah foresaw about Jerusalem:

*A day of the Lord is coming when your plunder will be divided among you.*

*I will gather all the nations to Jerusalem to fight against it; the city will be captured, the houses ransacked, and the women raped. Half of the city will go into exile, but the rest of the people will not be taken from the city (Zechariah 14:1,2).*

Just when the situation appears hopeless for the Jews living in Jerusalem, the picture will suddenly change. Jesus Christ will come down from heaven, setting His feet on the Mount of Olives. At that very instant a great earthquake will occur and the mountain will split in two. It will form a valley through which many Israelites will flee from their enemies. An eerie, dusk-like atmosphere will fall upon the Middle East, making daylight darker than usual and nighttime lighter. Water will begin to flow from Jerusalem toward the Dead Sea and the Mediterranean. We read:

> Then the Lord will go out and fight against those nations, as He fights in the day of battle. On that day His feet will stand on the Mount of Olives, east of Jerusalem, and the Mount of Olives will be split in two from east to west, forming a great valley, with half of the mountain moving north and half moving south. You will flee by My mountain valley, for it will extend to Azel. You will flee as you fled from the earthquake in the days of Uzziah king of Judah. Then the Lord my God will come, and all the holy ones with Him.
>
> On that day there will be no light, no cold or frost. It will be a unique day, without daytime or nighttime—a day known to the Lord. When evening comes, there will be light.
>
> On that day living water will flow out from Jerusalem, half to the eastern sea and half to the western sea, in summer and in winter.
>
> The Lord will be king over the whole earth. On that day there will be one Lord, and His name the only name (Zechariah 14:3-9).

Although these verses give us a good overall picture of the final stage of the war, we need to study Zechariah 12 and the rest of chapter 14 to get the details.

Before we do, however, let's review the setting. According to Daniel 11:40-45, the troops of Antichrist will be encamped on Mt. Zion between the Dead Sea and the Mediterranean. In Revelation 16:16 we read that the battle will begin in the Plain of Esdraelon in Galilee, just below the ancient fortress of Megiddo. Zechariah 14:1-9 tells us that the invading armies will enter Jerusalem, and that Christ will appear on the Mount of Olives just in the nick of time. As His feet touch the earth, a great earthquake will bring about tremendous topographical changes. The tide of battle will then change dramatically.

First, though many Israelites (perhaps mothers with

children and older people) will try to escape through
the valley opened by the splitting of the Mount of
Olives, others will be endowed with supernatural cour-
age and power. Zechariah wrote:

> *On that day I will make the leaders of Judah like a*
> *firepot in a woodpile, like a flaming torch among*
> *sheaves. They will consume right and left all the*
> *surrounding peoples, but Jerusalem will remain intact*
> *in her place.*
>
> *On that day the Lord will shield those who live in*
> *Jerusalem, so that the feeblest among them will be like*
> *David, and the house of David will be like God, like the*
> *Angel of the Lord going before them. On that day I will*
> *set out to destroy all the nations that attack Jerusalem*
> *(Zechariah 12:6,8,9).*

The Jewish people who will fight the enemy will undoubtedly be men and women who have been converted
through the great tribulation period. Perhaps they will
have hidden weapons for this occasion, or they may
seize the weapons of dead enemy soldiers. In any case,
they will experience the fulfillment of Psalm 91:7,8,
"A thousand may fall at your side, ten thousand at your
right hand, but it will not come near you. You will only
observe with your eyes and see the punishment of the
wicked."

Second, God will send a plague upon the enemy
soldiers, as we learn from these verses in Zechariah 14:

> *This is the plague with which the Lord will strike all the*
> *nations that fought against Jerusalem: Their flesh will*
> *rot while they are still standing on their feet, their eyes*
> *will rot in their sockets, and their tongues will rot in*
> *their mouths. . . . A similar plague will strike the horses*
> *and mules, the camels and donkeys, and all the*
> *animals in those camps (Zechariah 14:12,15).*

Third, the display of God's supernatural power, both in
the convolutions of nature and in the plagues, will
throw the surviving soldiers into such terror that they
will behave as if insane. Under the figure of oldtime
warfare conducted on horseback, the prophet drew the
following picture:

*"On that day I will strike every horse with panic and its rider with madness," declares the Lord. "I will keep a watchful eye over the house of Judah, but I will blind all the horses of the nations. Then the leaders of Judah will say in their hearts, 'The people of Jerusalem are strong, because the Lord Almighty is their God'"* (Zechariah 12:4,5).

*On that day men will be stricken by the Lord with great panic. Each man will seize the hand of another, and they will attack each other* (Zechariah 14:13).

Through all of these means, the invading armies will be completely destroyed and every soldier killed.

## THE GRAND FINALE

In the book of Revelation, the apostle John provided us with a beautiful portrait of Christ's second coming. He described it as the grand finale with these words:

*I saw heaven standing open and there before me was a white horse, whose rider is called Faithful and True. With justice He judges and makes war. His eyes are like blazing fire, and on His head are many crowns. He has a name written on Him that no one but He Himself knows. He is dressed in a robe dipped in blood, and His name is the Word of God. The armies of heaven were following Him, riding on white horses and dressed in fine linen, white and clean. Out of His mouth comes a sharp sword with which to strike down the nations. "He will rule them with an iron scepter." He treads the winepress of the fury of the wrath of God Almighty. On His robe and on His thigh He has this name written:*

*KING OF KINGS AND LORD OF LORDS.*

*And I saw an angel standing in the sun, who cried in a loud voice to all the birds flying in midair, "Come, gather together for the great supper of God, so that you may eat the flesh of kings, generals, and mighty men, of horses and their riders, and the flesh of all people, free and slave, small and great."*

*Then I saw the beast and the kings of the earth and their armies gathered together to make war against the rider on the horse and His army. But the beast was*

*performed the miraculous signs on his behalf. With
these signs he had deluded those who had received the
mark of the beast and worshiped his image. The two of
them were thrown alive into the fiery lake of burning
sulfur. The rest of them were killed with the sword that
came out of the mouth of the rider on the horse, and all
the birds gorged themselves on their flesh (Revelation
19:11-21).*

The symbolism is beautiful! John described Jesus
Christ descending from heaven on a white horse, followed by glorified saints in white garments and on
similar mounts. With the sword that issues from His
mouth He will destroy His enemies. He will throw the
beast and the false prophet "into the fiery lake of burning sulfur." Then, having overcome all His foes, Christ
will set in motion a program by which He will establish
the millennial kingdom.

This chart may help you see the chronology of the
endtime events which relate to the rule of Antichrist,
the destruction of Russia, and the war of Armageddon.

## DANIEL'S SEVENTIETH WEEK

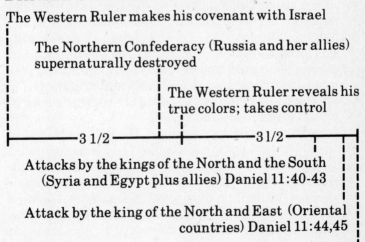

The Western Ruler makes his covenant with Israel

The Northern Confederacy (Russia and her allies)
supernaturally destroyed

The Western Ruler reveals his
true colors; takes control

|——————3 1/2 ——————|——————3 1/2 ——————|

Attacks by the kings of the North and the South
(Syria and Egypt plus allies) Daniel 11:40-43

Attack by the king of the North and East (Oriental
countries) Daniel 11:44,45

The Return of Christ in Glory

# 10. The Pre-kingdom Judgments

The last few years before Christ returns in glory will feature a spectacular display of the supernatural. The invisible conflict of the ages will finally be brought out in the open. The power of God and of Satan will be manifested throughout the world. Everyone will be forced to choose between good and evil in those perilous days. It is therefore fitting that when the great tribulation is ended and the kingdom age is about to begin, a series of divine court sessions will be held.

Jesus Christ will sit as Judge. He will be bringing into account two groups of people: (1) The resurrected believers from the ages prior to Pentecost and the saints who were martyred during the tribulation. They will be judged before Christ exactly as were the raptured saints of the church age. (2) Those believers who will live through the great tribulation. According to Isaiah this will be a relatively small number, for a great percentage of the people who are alive when the tribulation began will have perished.

*Therefore a curse consumes the earth; its people must
bear their guilt. Therefore earth's inhabitants are
burned up, and very few are left (Isaiah 24:6).*

## PRE-KINGDOM JUDGMENT IN HEAVEN

Before the Lord Jesus ascends the throne of David to
rule over the earth, He will call all of His redeemed and
glorified saints to personal account. Paul declared:

*For we must all appear before the judgment seat of
Christ, that each one may receive what is due him for
the things done while in the body, whether good or bad
(2 Corinthians 5:10).*

Immediately after believers receive their resurrection
bodies, they will stand before Christ for a personal
accounting. Let us look carefully at what the Bible
teaches about the time, the question, the standard, and
the result of the judgment seat of Christ.

*The Time.* All the believers of the pre-kingdom
ages—church saints, Old Testament believers, and
tribulation martyrs—will appear before the Lord Jesus
for judgment during the period between the rapture
and the beginning of the millennium. But they will not
appear simultaneously.

The saints of the church age—those people who are
saved during the interval between Pentecost and the
rapture—will receive their resurrection bodies and be
judged by Christ *before* the great tribulation begins. In
a previous chapter we saw that "the man of lawlessness" cannot be fully manifested until the Holy Spirit
in His function of restraining sin through the church is
taken "out of the way" (2 Thessalonians 2:3,7). I believe the resurrected and raptured believers of the
church age will be judged in the air while the tribulation is beginning on the earth. That the church, the
bride of Christ, will be judged at this time is confirmed
by the picture given in Revelation 19:6 through 8.

*Then I heard what sounded like a great multitude, like
the roar of rushing waters and like loud peals of
thunder, shouting: "Hallelujah! For our Lord God
Almighty reigns. Let us rejoice and be glad and give*

*Him glory! For the wedding of the Lamb has come, and*
*His bride has made herself ready. Fine linen, bright*
*and clean, was given her to wear." (Fine linen stands*
*for the righteous acts of the saints.)*

The fact that the bride has been made ready and is
dressed in fine linen indicates that the judgment of
believers will have already taken place when Christ
returns in glory.

The saved of the Old Testament era will be resurrected and judged right *after* the great tribulation. We
read about their resurrection in Daniel's prophecy.

*At that time Michael, the great prince who protects your*
*people, will arise. There will be a time of distress such*
*as has not happened from the beginning of nations until*
*then. But at that time your people—everyone whose*
*name is found written in the book—will be delivered.*
*Multitudes who sleep in the dust of the earth will*
*awake: some to everlasting life, others to shame and*
*everlasting contempt. Those who are wise will shine*
*like the brightness of the heavens, and those who lead*
*many to righteousness, like the stars for ever and ever*
*(Daniel 12:1-3).*

Dr. Leon Wood, respected Old Testament scholar,
suggested that the Hebrew expression with which
these verses open, "at that time," should be translated
"during that time." Michael, the archangel who has
been given a special ministry to Israel, will be active
during the great tribulation. He will make certain that
a chosen remnant of Jewish people is spared to enter
the millennium in their earthly bodies.

God will remember His promises to national Israel,
and He will fulfill them. But He will also remember the
godly whose bodies have returned to the elements.
"Multitudes who sleep in the dust of the earth will
awake: some to everlasting life . . ." (Daniel 12:2). The
Hebrew text carefully distinguishes between two
groups who will be resurrected—one to "everlasting
life," and the other at a later time "to shame and
everlasting contempt." The believing dead of Old
Testament times, therefore, will receive their glorified

bodies at the close of the great tribulation. They will appear at the judgment seat of Christ just before our Lord establishes His kingdom over the earth.

Interestingly, the prophet Daniel implied that an interval of 45 days will occur between the time of Christ's coming at Armageddon and the establishment of the millennial kingdom. He first declared that 1,290 days will elapse between the moment Antichrist desecrates the Jewish temple and the time of Christ's glorious return. Then he pronounced a blessing upon those people who will still be on earth 45 days later— presumably to enter the kingdom age. Apparently our Lord will spend 45 days holding court sessions, making appointments, and organizing His cabinet. We read:

> *From the time that the daily sacrifice is abolished and the abomination that causes desolation is set up, there will be 1,290 days. Blessed is the one who waits for and reaches the end of the 1,335 days (Daniel 12:11,12).*

The martyrs of the great tribulation will also be resurrected and judged during this 45-day interval. The apostle John wrote about their resurrection in Revelation 20.

> *I saw thrones on which were seated those who had been given authority to judge. And I saw the souls of those who had been beheaded because of their testimony for Jesus and because of the word of God. They had not worshiped the beast or his image and had not received his mark on their foreheads or their hands. They came to life and reigned with Christ a thousand years. (The rest of the dead did not come to life until the thousand years were ended.) This is the first resurrection. Blessed and holy are those who have part in the first resurrection. The second death has no power over them, but they will be priests of God and of Christ and will reign with Him for a thousand years (Revelation 20:4-6).*

Notice that John saw one company already seated on thrones and possessing authority to judge. These are the church saints in their glorified bodies. He also observed a group who were not yet in their new bodies—the "souls of those who had been beheaded because of their testimony for Jesus." He carefully identified them as those who "had not worshiped the beast or his image and had not received his mark on their foreheads or their hands." Obviously these are martyrs of the great tribulation. As John observed the scene, these "souls" suddenly "came to life"; that is, they received their resurrection bodies. The apostle didn't mention their judgment, but because every believer must appear at the judgment seat of Christ we may assume that they will do so at approximately the same time as the Old Testament believers.

In summary, church saints, Old Testament believers, and the martyrs of the great tribulation will all appear at the judgment seat of Christ. Believers from the church age will receive their glorified bodies and be judged before the great tribulation begins. Old Testament believers and great tribulation martyrs will be resurrected and judged during the interval between our Lord's descent to the Mount of Olives and His actual occupation of the throne in Jerusalem.

*The Question.* The issue to be settled at the judgment seat of Christ will be the measure of the reward each person receives. The question will not be whether they go to heaven or hell. Everyone who stands at the judgment seat of Christ is a sinner saved by grace and will already be in heaven. The Lord Jesus will call each of us to give an account of our service as His bondslave. He's going to examine the quality of our devotion during our earthly sojourn. "For we must all appear before the judgment seat of Christ, that each one may receive *what is due him* for the things done while in the body, whether good or bad" (2 Corinthians 5:10).

*The Standard.* The standard of judgment will be our faithfulness. Some people with great accomplishments may receive relatively few rewards because they have squandered many opportunities and wasted their abilities. Paul declared, "Now it is required that those who have been given a trust prove *faithful.* . . . It is the Lord who judges me" (1 Corinthians 4:2,4).

Jesus emphasized the matter of faithfulness in three parables—the workers in the vineyard (Matthew 20:1-16), the talents (Matthew 25:14-30), and the pounds (Luke 19:11-27). It isn't how long we serve the Lord or how much we accomplish that really counts—it is faithfulness! Our Lord summarized this truth as follows: "From everyone who has been given much, much will be demanded; and from the one who has been entrusted with much, much more will be asked" (Luke 12:48).

*The Result.* The result of the judgment seat of Christ will be that some receive "reward" as they enter eternity in their glorified bodies, while others suffer "loss." We have difficulty comprehending exactly what is involved in this "reward" or "loss" because we can't visualize life under perfect conditions. We do know, however, that the "loss" will not involve punishment. That was borne by Jesus on the cross. We should therefore banish from our minds any thought of a punitive process or a time of purgatory.

The loss associated with the judgment seat of Christ will undoubtedly involve the pain of regret and shame. Even though Jesus took all the punishment for our sins and will not remind us of the shortcomings we have confessed and forsaken, He likely will call to our attention those sins we never confessed and the wrongs we never made right. He may cause us to see how selfish we were even in some of the good things we did. How ashamed we will be! John's admonition is appropriate: "And now, dear children, continue in Him, so that when He appears we may be confident and unashamed before Him at His coming" (1 John 2:28). I clearly remember the shame I felt as a boy when a teacher I admired confronted me about my wrong attitude toward another person. This makes me realize that one can suffer much pain without corporal punishment.

The loss will also be expressed in the degree of our reward. I believe that some will enter their eternal state with less glory than others. People have a hard time accepting this idea because they think it would bring unhappiness into heaven. I don't agree. The fact that there will be differing degrees of glory is not incompatible with complete happiness for all. Every person in heaven will be satisfied that Jesus Christ was absolutely fair. Not one of us will be envious of another. We will all agree that we were saved by grace alone from the hell we deserved. Right now I'm perfectly happy with my Chevrolet—even when I see a friend in his new Mercedes. And I'm still a sinner! If I can feel that way on earth, I can be assured that I'll never be envious of others up there. We'll all shine. It's just a matter of some shining more brightly than others. We'll all be perfectly happy.

In summary, before Jesus sets up His kingdom on earth, He will sit at His seat of judgment to examine the quality of the lives of all His redeemed and resurrected people. We of the church age will appear there as the tribulation period begins on earth. Old Testament believers and great tribulation martyrs will stand there later—during the 45-day interval between Christ's return and His ascension to the throne in Jerusalem. Jesus Christ will assess every life. The standard for all will be faithfulness. The eternal result will be varying degrees of glory.

## JUDGMENTS ON EARTH

In addition to judging the glorified saints above, Jesus will hold two judgments on earth for the people who survive the great tribulation. The evidence indicates that He will also do this during the 45-day interval to which we already referred. Christ will examine both Jews and Gentiles to determine who will be allowed entrance into His kingdom.

*Earth-dwelling Jews.* The prophet Ezekiel used the figure of a shepherd checking out his sheep as they enter the fold to portray the Lord as He examines each Israelite to determine whether or not he or she is eligible for entrance into the kingdom. In some manner not revealed, God will call to account every Jew who survives the great tribulation. He will cause some to die

and depart into Hades, and He will let others live to
become citizens of the kingdom. Here is how Ezekiel
portrayed this judgment:

> *As surely as I live, declares the Sovereign Lord, I will*
> *rule over you with a mighty hand and an out-*
> *stretched arm and with outpoured wrath. I will bring*
> *you from the nations and gather you from the countries*
> *where you have been scattered—with a mighty hand*
> *and an outstretched arm and with outpoured wrath. I*
> *will bring you into the desert of the nations and there,*
> *face to face, I will execute judgment upon you. As I*
> *judged your fathers in the desert of the land of Egypt, so*
> *I will judge you, declares the Sovereign Lord. I will take*
> *note of you as you pass under My staff, and I will bring*
> *you into the bond of the covenant. I will purge you of*
> *those who revolt and rebel against Me. Although I will*
> *bring them out of the land where they are living, yet they*
> *will not enter the land of Israel. Then you will know*
> *that I am the Lord.*
>
> *As for you, O house of Israel, this is what the*
> *Sovereign Lord says: Go and serve your idols, every one*
> *of you! But afterward you will surely listen to Me and*
> *no longer profane My holy name with your gifts and*
> *idols. For on My holy mountain, the high mountain of*
> *Israel, declares the Sovereign Lord, there in the land*
> *the entire house of Israel will serve Me, and there I will*
> *accept them. There I will require your offerings and*
> *your choice gifts, along with all your holy sacrifices*
> *(Ezekiel 20:33-44).*

Remember, every Jew involved in this judgment will
have gone through the great tribulation. It is safe to
assume that every one of them will have made a decision about Jesus Christ. Some of them will be Christ's
enemies, for they will have decided to join Antichrist in
his revolt against God. These rebels will be put to
death. However, the Jews who accept Christ and refuse
to worship the beast or his image will enter the
millennium. Apart from children not old enough to be
morally accountable, all the Jews who enter the kingdom will be firm believers in the Lord Jesus as Savior.

*Living Gentiles.* The second pre-kingdom earthly judgment will be for the Gentiles who will have survived the great tribulation. It will occur in the same time frame as the judgment of the Jews. Here is our Lord's description of it:

*When the Son of Man comes in His glory, and all the angels with Him, He will sit on His throne in heavenly glory. All the nations will be gathered before Him, and He will separate the people one from another as a shepherd separates the sheep from the goats. He will put the sheep on His right and the goats on His left.*

*Then the King will say to those on His right, "Come, you who are blessed by My Father; take your inheritance, the kingdom prepared for you since the creation of the world. For I was hungry and you gave Me something to eat, I was thirsty and you gave Me something to drink, I was a stranger and you invited Me in, I needed clothes and you clothed Me, I was sick and you looked after Me, I was in prison and you came to visit Me."*

*Then the righteous will answer Him, "Lord, when did we see You hungry and feed You, or thirsty and give You something to drink? When did we see You a stranger and invite You in, or needing clothes and clothe You? When did we see You sick or in prison and go to visit You?"*

*The King will reply, "I tell you the truth, whatever you did for one of the least of these brothers of Mine, you did for Me."*

*Then He will say to those on His left, "Depart from Me, you who are cursed, into the eternal fire prepared for the devil and his angels. For I was hungry and you gave Me nothing to eat, I was thirsty and you gave Me nothing to drink, I was a stranger and you did not invite Me in, I needed clothes and you did not clothe Me, I was sick and in prison and you did not look after Me."*

*They also will answer, "Lord, when did we see You hungry or thirsty or a stranger or needing clothes or sick or in prison, and did not help You?"*

*He will reply, "I tell you the truth, whatever you did*

*not do for one of the least of these, you did not do*
*for Me."*
    *Then they will go away to eternal punishment, but*
*the righteous to eternal life (Matthew 25:31-46).*

This is a judgment of individuals, not of nations. Nations as such do not go into eternal punishment or eternal life. The issue will be the same as that of the judgment depicted in Ezekiel 20, and the result will be either death or entrance into the millennium. At the judgment, the Gentiles will be commended and rewarded for the love they showed Christ's "brethren" during the great tribulation. They will have taken great risks to do so because of their faith in Christ. Some Gentiles during this terrible time apparently will worship the beast, but they will refrain from persecuting the Jews. They will discover that their so-called neutrality was not pleasing to the Lord. All the unbelieving will die immediately. It appears that among Gentiles, as among Jews, only genuine believers in Jesus Christ will enter the kingdom. (The exception again will be children not yet morally accountable.)

In conclusion, when Jesus Christ comes again, He will resurrect and judge His people. He will glorify and evaluate the lives of church-age saints before He allows Antichrist to be revealed. He will glorify and judge Old Testament believers and tribulation saints after He descends in glory, and while He is preparing for His rule over the earth. During this time He will also hold court sessions on earth to purge out all unbelievers, so that only believers enter the 1,000-year kingdom.

Admittedly, we have a difficult time visualizing these judgments. We tend to think of individuals standing in long lines, each awaiting his turn. This process would require many, many years. Because Jesus Christ is God as well as man, He will judge all mankind simultaneously. Yet each believer will be conscious of a personal encounter with Him. And, because Christ's judgment is right and true, all will be satisfied with the outcome.

How wonderful to have the assurance that Jesus paid the complete price for all our sins on the cross! Every believer, whether saved during the first era of human history, during the millennium, and every period of time between, can look forward without fear of punishment.

I know some elderly Christians who live in fear because they can't overcome deep guilt feelings over sins they committed when young. They have placed their trust in the Lord Jesus, but somehow they can't bring themselves to believe that their sins are totally wiped off the record. But that's what God's Word declares! Just before Jesus sent forth His spirit in death, He called out loudly "It is finished." It was a shout of victory! He had paid the full price for our redemption! When we accept Him as our Savior, we are totally and completely pardoned. We stand before the Lord as clean as the newly driven snow. That's what Paul had in mind when he wrote the words, "Therefore, since we have been justified through faith, we have peace with God through our Lord Jesus Christ..." (Romans 5:1).

The thought of judgment is solemn. But it need not be frightening for a child of God.

# 11. The Millennial Kingdom

When I was a boy, my family went to a church where The Lord's Prayer was recited in unison every Sunday. I still recall the thoughts that went through my mind when we repeated the words, "Thy kingdom come. Thy will be done in earth, as it is in heaven." I wondered why Jesus included this petition in His prayer, for our church taught that the time would never come when the will of God would be done on this earth as it is done in heaven. Besides, I was firmly convinced that moral and spiritual conditions would deteriorate until Christ would return to destroy our earth-system and usher in eternity. I realized, of course, that some Christians talked about a golden age of 1,000 years at the close of human history, but I dismissed this concept as being nothing more than a wistful dream.

I had some questions about this, however. For one thing, I noted that the Old Testament prophecies were specific when speaking about a time when the Messiah

115

would rule over the earth and bring peace, prosperity, righteousness, and blessedness to all mankind. These passages said that Jerusalem would be the earth's capital city, and that Israel would become the central nation. Yet I had been taught that these prophecies and promises would not be literally fulfilled, because the nation of Israel had rejected Christ when He came. I also believed that our Lord's death on the cross had abolished all distinctions between Jew and Gentile, and that Israel would never again hold a special place in God's program. Therefore, I told myself that the prophecies about an earthly kingdom had to be interpreted as symbols of the spiritual blessings the Lord's people would one day realize in heaven.

Today I take a different position. I firmly believe that Christ will rule over a literal, earthly kingdom of peace and righteousness, and that Israel will be given a place of priority in it. I am convinced that most Jewish people will be converted to faith in Christ during the coming great tribulation, and that they will welcome Him when He returns. I fully expect Jerusalem to be the world capital from which Jesus Christ will rule all mankind. We refer to this golden age as the millennium because Revelation 20 tells us that it will last a thousand years.

In this chapter, I will explain in detail some of the outstanding features of this coming kingdom age. I hope I will be able to sweep away the common misconceptions and extol the beauty of God's redemptive plan for the earth and mankind.

## A PERFECT KING

The first feature of the millennial kingdom will be its perfect King. None other than Jesus Christ will rule. He will fulfill Jeremiah's prophecy:

*"The days are coming," declares the Lord, "when I will raise up to David a righteous Branch, a King who will reign wisely and do what is just and right in the land.*

*"In His days Judah will be saved and Israel will live*

*in safety. This is the name by which He will be called:*
*The Lord Our Righteousness" (Jeremiah 23:5,6).*

Christ's coming to reign will also bring to fulfillment the prediction the angel made to Mary when he announced that she would become the mother of the Messiah.

*He will be great and will be called the Son of the Most*
*High. The Lord God will give Him the throne of His*
*father David, and He will reign over the house of Jacob*
*forever; His kingdom will never end (Luke 1:32,33).*

The prediction that Jesus Christ will be the King of the earth doesn't raise serious objections, in and of itself. Many Bible students are troubled, however, by certain characteristics the prophets said will be part of His rule. Some resent its "Jewishness"—the oft-repeated declaration that Jerusalem will be the capital of His kingdom and Israel the central nation. Others are offended by the prophetic portrayal of our Lord as a totalitarian ruler who will establish harsh, restrictive, and dictatorial policies. Therefore, let's look more closely at these aspects of His kingdom rule.

*The Jewishness of the Millennial Kingdom.* Beyond question, the prophets saw Israel as the central nation of the millennium, Jerusalem as its capital, and David's throne as its seat of authority. The importance of Israel and Jerusalem in this coming kingdom is set forth vividly by Isaiah:

*This is what Isaiah son of Amoz saw concerning Judah*
*and Jerusalem: In the last days the mountain of the*
*Lord's temple will be established as chief among the*
*mountains; it will be raised above the hills, and all*
*nations will stream to it. Many peoples will come and*
*say, "Come, let us go up to the mountain of the Lord, to*
*the house of the God of Jacob. He will teach us His ways,*
*so that we may walk in His paths." The law will go out*
*from Zion, the word of the Lord from Jerusalem*
*(Isaiah 2:1-3).*

The glory of Jerusalem during the millennial age is declared with exquisite beauty in the following passage:

*Foreigners will rebuild your walls, and their kings will serve you. Though in anger I struck you, in favor I will show you compassion. Your gates will always stand open, they will never be shut, day or night, so that men may bring you the wealth of the nations—their kings led in triumphal procession. For the nation or kingdom that will not serve you will perish; it will be utterly ruined. The glory of Lebanon will come to you, the pine, the fir, and the cypress together, to adorn the place of My sanctuary; and I will glorify the place of My feet. The sons of your oppressors will come bowing before you; all who despise you will bow down at your feet and will call you The City of the Lord, Zion of the Holy One of Israel (Isaiah 60:10-14).*

As Lord of lords and King of kings, Jesus Christ will reign over mankind from "the throne of His father David" (Luke 1:32). Because the first throne of David was on earth, we must conclude that David's most illustrious successor will also rule from the city of Jerusalem.

Does this mean that Jesus will leave heaven and live on earth day and night in His glorified body, as He did during the 33 years of His earthly ministry? I don't think so. He certainly will not divest Himself of His heavenly body. I expect Him to commute between heaven and earth, much like He did during the 40 days between His resurrection and ascension. It is possible that He will choose a descendant of David as His vice-regent to carry out many of the functions associated with the office. But He will be the actual, literal King, ruling all earth from Jerusalem.

I don't see why this should be considered impossible or unlikely. After all, God called Israel out to be a special nation. He made this people the receptacle of special revelation and the vehicle through whom Christ would come. He deeded the land of Palestine to them. He told them repeatedly that if they obeyed Him, He would exalt them in a coming golden age of universal peace, prosperity, and blessedness. Then He set the nation aside during the church age. In Romans, Paul told the Jews that God had a perfect right to do this. After all, He's God. But this same God also has the prerogative to bring about the nation's conversion to Christ, restoring them so that they can fulfill the unique role He has chosen for them.

*The Dictatorial Nature of Christ's Kingdom.* What about the accusation that we make the Lord a totalitarian authority in this coming kingdom? Will He really be an absolute dictator who will permit no opposition? Absolutely! We have already seen that when He establishes His kingdom, He will destroy His enemies. Only believers will be allowed to enter the millennium! And He will insist upon continued loyalty as new generations of people come on the scene. When He selects new leaders for the exploding population, He will choose only people who are outwardly loyal to Him. Then, when some of these people reveal their heart opposition by trying to instigate rebellion, He will deal with them forcibly. The writer of Psalm 2 portrayed the millennial King's reponse to rebellion as follows:

*I will proclaim the decree of the Lord: He said to Me, "You are My Son; today I have become Your Father. Ask of Me, and I will make the nations Your inheritance, the ends of the earth Your possession. You will rule them with an iron scepter; You will dash them to pieces like pottery. Therefore, you kings, be wise; be warned, you rulers of the earth. Serve the Lord with fear and rejoice with trembling. Kiss the Son, lest He be angry and you be destroyed in your way, for His wrath can flare up in a moment. Blessed are all who take refuge in Him" (Psalm 2:7-12).*

Yes, Jesus will be an absolute dictator. He will displace one of our cherished freedoms—that of religion. He will not permit the practice or propagation of false religion in any form. After all, every belief-system that doesn't give Him His rightful place can only lead to eternal death. He spoke the truth when He said shortly before His crucifixion, "I am the way and the truth and the life. No one comes to the Father except through Me" (John 14:6). Since Jesus is the only way to God, He would be remiss in carrying out His duties if He were to let evil or deluded people proclaim ideas that could only bring harm to those who accept them.

We today cherish religious freedom, and rightly so. Our rulers are imperfect, fallible people. They are not wise enough or good enough to be given absolute authority over every area of life. But Jesus Christ, the sinless Son of God, possesses a combination of goodness, wisdom, and power that qualifies Him to exercise absolute authority over every area of human life and behavior. Besides, He is the Maker and Sustainer: the End of all existence. "For by Him all things were created: things in heaven and on earth, visible and invisible, whether thrones or powers or rulers or authorities; all things were created by Him and for Him. He is before all things, and in Him all things hold together" (Colossians 1:16,17). How can anybody object to His taking over earth's government?

The results of Christ's rule will be astonishing. He will bring about peace between the nations. Prosperity, righteousness, and justice will be given to all. The prophets wrote:

*He will judge between the nations and will settle disputes for many peoples. They will beat their swords into plowshares and their spears into pruning hooks. Nation will not take up sword against nation, nor will they train for war anymore (Isaiah 2:4).*

*Every man will sit under his own vine and under his own fig tree, and no one will make them afraid, for the Lord Almighty has spoken (Micah 4:4).*

Jesus Christ will achieve the dreams of good rulers—a perfect balance between kindness and firmness. He will not let the wealthy and powerful exploit hardworking people from lower levels of society. But He won't tolerate social parasites either. We read:

*They will build houses and dwell in them; they will plant vineyards and eat their fruit. No longer will they build houses and others live in them, or plant and others eat. For as the days of a tree, so will be the days of My people; My chosen ones will long enjoy the works of*

*their hands. They will not toil in vain or bear children
doomed to misfortune; for they will be a people blessed
by the Lord, they and their descendants with them
(Isaiah 65:21-23).*

In summary, Jesus Christ will rule as an absolute
monarch. He will put down all rebellion. He will prevent wars between the nations. He will protect the
weak from being exploited by the strong. He will deal
firmly with the lazy and shiftless who want to get by
without working. He will demand that all mankind
worship the true and living God, and He will forbid the
teaching and practice of all false religions. The one
thing He won't do, however, is force people to believe in
their hearts. He will respect man's free will to choose
his eternal destiny.

## A TRANSFORMED NATURAL WORLD

A second feature of this millennial kingdom will be *a
transformed natural world.* This earth will be a far
more beautiful and delightful place than it is today.
The deserts are too hot and dry. Jungle regions are too
wet and humid; Alaska and Siberia are too cold.
Earthquakes, volcanoes, hurricanes, and tornadoes kill
and injure thousands every year. Periods of drought
cause food shortages and starvation. Insects make life
miserable for man and beast. Plague and disease bring
premature death to many thousands. Birth defects prevent large numbers from ever experiencing the blessings of a normal life.

If you and your family are healthy and live in the
right part of the world, you think of this earth as a
pretty good place. Even the desolate areas of our planet
may hold beauty for you when you view them from an
airplane or an air-conditioned automobile.

But if you are a sensitive and thoughtful person, you
can't help being painfully aware of the fact that our
world has much about it that is far from beautiful. Animals are forced to endure a great deal of suffering.
Some die from starvation during the cold winter
months and others are devoured by predators. The

stinging bites of flies and mosquitos and the distress caused by ticks and mites must also be endured. Millions upon millions of people are crowded into densely populated cities where they live in rat-infested tenements and go hungry, while acres and acres of land are uninhabitable. Yes, under the curse, nature isn't very kind. But during the coming millennium, conditions will be far different. God will bring about tremendous changes that will alter weather conditions, the nature of animals, and the health and longevity of mankind. Let's think about these changes more specifically.

*Changes in Climate.* In the millennium, God is going to do something about the weather. He will bring rainfall to areas now bone dry most of the time, and He will cause the sun to send more heat to some parts of the earth. The result will be an abundance of food, enough for man and beast. The prophet Isaiah declared:

*He will also send you rain for the seed you sow in the ground, and the food that comes from the land will be rich and plentiful. In that day your cattle will graze in broad meadows. The oxen and donkeys that work the soil will eat fodder and mash, spread out with fork and shovel. In the day of great slaughter, when the towers fall, streams of water will flow on every high mountain and every lofty hill. The moon will shine like the sun, and the sunlight will be seven times brighter, like the light of seven full days, when the Lord binds up the bruises of His people and heals the wounds He inflicted (Isaiah 30:23-26).*

*Then will the lame leap like a deer, and the tongue of the dumb shout for joy. Water will gush forth in the wilderness and streams in the desert. The burning sand will become a pool, the thirsty ground bubbling springs. In the haunts where jackals once lay, grass and reeds and papyrus will grow (Isaiah 35:6,7).*

All of the abundance of food produced under these conditions will be properly administrated and distributed. King Jesus will see to that!

*Changes in the Animal World.* The Old Testament prophets indicated that the nature of animals will be profoundly changed. Wild animals will no longer be a threat to humans. We read:

> In that day I will make a covenant for them with the beasts of the field and the birds of the air and the creatures that move along the ground (Hosea 2:18).

A new harmony within the animal kingdom will also become evident.

> The wolf will live with the lamb, the leopard will lie down with the goat, the calf and the lion and the yearling together; and a little child will lead them. The cow will feed with the bear, their young will lie down together, and the lion will eat straw like the ox. The infant will play near the hole of the cobra, and the young child put his hand into the viper's nest (Isaiah 11:6-8).

This passage has been the center of a great deal of discussion. The amillennialists view it as a symbolic description of either the harmony of heaven or the spiritual peace that comes to those who accept the Messiah. But these interpretations violate the context and rob this beautiful passage of any real meaning.

Delitzsch, the brilliant German textual scholar, commented on promises of this kind as follows:

> This also is not meant figuratively. . . . It is not of the new heaven that the prophet is speaking, but of the glorification of nature, which is promised by both Old Testament prophecy and by that of the New at the closing period of the world's history. . . . No other miracles will be needed for this than that wonder-working power of God. . . . Heaven and earth will then put on their sabbath dress, for it will be the Sabbath of the world's history (*Commentary on Isaiah,* translated by J. Martin, Eerdman's Publishing Company, Grand Rapids, 1950, Vol. 2, p. 39).

Premillennial scholars generally take this passage to mean exactly what it says. They are convinced that God is going to change the nature of carnivorous animals. Lions, leopards, bears, and wolves will be changed so drastically that they will eat grass. Those who take this passage literally realize that to be consistent they must conclude that the whole present order will be changed. Owls and cats will no longer kill rodents. Purple martins and swallows will no longer eat insects. God will either let all obnoxious and destructive creatures die off, or He will change the species so much that it will in no way be a pest. This view raises many questions. Will no insects or animals die? If not, will the Lord simply stop all insect and animal reproduction when their population reaches the saturation point?

Though I am a literalist and do not doubt God's ability to perform the tremendous changes I just suggested, I do not think it necessary to insist that lions and leopards are going to get new mouths and digestive systems. I am not at all sure that porcupines will get soft fur or that skunks will spray cologne. It seems to me that we should take Isaiah's words as a portrait of the new conditions on earth. They will extend even to the animal world. The prophet may be employing this picture as a literary device to show us that children and domesticated animals will be perfectly safe in this coming age. This metaphoric form of speech isn't unusual. Joel declared:

*In that day the mountains will drip new wine, and the hills will flow with milk (Joel 3:18).*

I see this as figurative language depicting an abundance of new wine and milk—representative of great prosperity. People won't literally stand with pails at the side of a mountain to catch dripping grape juice or milk. They will still obtain these products from vineyards and cows.

Remember, the millennium will take place upon this earth, and its citizens will be flesh-and-blood human beings. People will still have a sinful nature; therefore, everything won't be perfect. But with a perfect Ruler who brings peace, prosperity, righteousness, and greatly altered natural conditions, life will be filled with joy and delight.

I've never lost any sleep over the thought that a trout

eats minnows or that some of my friends catch fish. In fact, fishing will be great during the millennium.

*Swarms of living creatures will live wherever the river flows. There will be large numbers of fish, because this water flows there and makes the salt water fresh; so where the river flows everything will live. Fishermen will stand along the shore; from En Gedi to En Eglaim there will be places for spreading nets. The fish will be of many kinds — like the fish of the Great Sea (Ezekiel 47:9,10).*

In summary, God will one day bring about great changes in the animal world. Humans and their domesticated animals will have nothing to fear from venomous creatures or wild, flesh-eating beasts. The Lord will either drastically alter their whole structure so that no creature eats another, or He will bring about such a perfect balance that all pests are brought under control.

*Changes in Health and Longevity.* During the millennial age people will enjoy far better health than they do now, and they will live much longer. In fact, it appears that as the millennium begins all who have a weak or handicapped body will be made well.

*Then will the eyes of the blind be opened and the ears of the deaf unstopped. Then will the lame leap like a deer, and the tongue of the dumb shout for joy (Isaiah 35:5,6).*

As the age continues, all infants will be born in healthy bodies and grow to maturity. Death will be the exception rather than the rule. Very likely only those who have been willfully disobedient to Christ will die. A person who is 100 years old will be considered young.

*I will rejoice over Jerusalem and take delight in My people; the sound of weeping and of crying will be heard in it no more. Never again will there be in it an infant that lives but a few days, or an old man who does not live out his years; he who dies at a hundred will be thought a mere youth; he who fails to reach a hundred will be considered accursed. No longer will they build houses and others live in them, or plant and others eat.*

*For as the days of a tree, so will be the days of My*
*people; My chosen ones will long enjoy the works of*
*their hands (Isaiah 65:19,20,22).*

The prophet's comparison of the human lifespan with a
tree reminds me of a maple that stands alongside a
road near where I lived when I was about 12 years old.
I hated walking by it at nighttime because I was
always afraid that someone would be lurking behind it.
It was old and large then. Recently, 50 years later, I
saw it again. Although it has grown during the intervening years, it looks the same to me now as it did when
I was a youngster. Unless someone cuts it down, it's
likely to continue standing there for generations to
come. The tree therefore serves as an accurate symbol
of long life.

In addition, trees will be a source of food and medicine during the millennium.

*Fruit trees of all kinds will grow on both banks of the*
*river. Their leaves will not wither, nor will their fruit*
*fail. Every month they will bear, because the water*
*from the sanctuary flows to them. Their fruit will serve*
*for food and their leaves for healing (Ezekiel 47:12).*

The mention of fruit for food and leaves for healing
brings to mind the story of Adam and Eve after the fall.
One of the reasons God banished our first parents from
the garden of Eden was to keep them from eating the
fruit of the tree of life. It appears that if they could
have continued eating its fruit they would have kept on
living. Ezekiel seems to be telling us that the fruit and
leaves of certain trees will provide nourishing food and
healing medication for earth's citizens throughout the
millennium.

Natural conditions on the earth during the kingdom
age will be quite different from what they are at
present. The upheaval of mountain ranges and drastic
cosmic changes will cause desert wastelands to become
garden spots. The whole earth will be blessed with
moderate temperatures and adequate rainfall. Wild
animals will live harmoniously with mankind and
offer no threat to domesticated beasts. Everyone who

obeys Jesus Christ will enjoy good health and probably live through the entire thousand-year period.

## A MANDATED RELIGION

Another feature of the millennial age will be a single, mandated religious system. The temple in Jerusalem will be its worship center. I know that this statement will raise some eyebrows. A temple in Jerusalem as the center of worship? That smacks of ancient Judaism! Especially when we interpet literally the concluding eight chapters of Ezekiel. This passage delineates the tribal areas that will be assigned to the Israelites, depicts a new priesthood, and tells about sacrifices that will be offered in the temple.

I am well aware of these objections. I raised them myself when I was still an amillennialist, and I believe they should be answered. I will do so by stating three simple propositions and explaining them. First, during the millennial age true faith will be a matter of the heart just as it is today. Second, the worship of the Lord will be universal just as it is now. Third, the sacrifices will be commemorative, much like baptism and the Lord's Supper are today.

*A Heart Religion.* As the priest-king in the millennial age, Christ will not permit the practice and propagation of false religions, and He will make certain demands on all people. Mere outward conformity will not be enough, for true religion will still be a matter of the heart. In fact, the Jewish people will possess an "inwardized" faith far beyond anything ever experienced in their previous history. They will be living under what the prophet Jeremiah called their "new covenant." We read:

> "This is the covenant I will make with the house of Israel after that time," declares the Lord. "I will put My law in their minds and write it on their hearts. I will be their God, and they will be My people. No longer will a man teach his neighbor, or a man his brother, saying, 'Know the Lord,' because they will all know Me, from the least of them to the greatest," declares the Lord.

*"For I will forgive their wickedness and will remember their sins no more" (Jeremiah 31:33,34).*

The true believers on earth during this coming age, whether Jew or Gentile, will experience the presence and power of the Holy Spirit the same way the disciples did on the Day of Pentecost. At that time the apostle Peter told his Jewish audience that they were witnessing the beginning of the age of the Spirit predicted by the prophet Joel:

*And afterward, I will pour out My Spirit on all people. Your sons and daughters will prophesy, your old men will dream dreams, your young men will see visions. Even on My servants, both men and women, I will pour out My Spirit in those days. I will show wonders in the heavens and on the earth, blood and fire and billows of smoke. The sun will be turned to darkness and the moon to blood before the coming of the great and dreadful day of the Lord. And everyone who calls on the name of the Lord will be saved; for on Mount Zion and in Jerusalem there will be deliverance, as the Lord has said, among the survivors whom the Lord calls (Joel 2:28-32).*

In the millennium, believers will enjoy all the blessings associated with the coming of the Holy Spirit on Pentecost. They will know the power of a Spirit-filled life. They won't be subjected to many of the temptations and trials that they experience today because the devil will be bound, and illness, persecution, and poverty will be absent. Even so, they will face the temptations that come through affluence. How easy it will be to become proud and self-sufficient under such circumstances!

Remember, when the kingdom age begins, all of its citizens (except small children) will be born-again people. The prophet Ezekiel declared:

*I will sprinkle clean water on you, and you will be clean; I will cleanse you from all your impurities and from all your idols. I will give you a new heart and put a new spirit in you; I will remove from you your heart of stone and give you a heart of flesh. And I will put My*

*Spirit in you and move you to follow My decrees and be*
*careful to keep My laws (Ezekiel 36:25-28).*

As succeeding generations come on the scene, each
person will be called upon to believe on Christ—just as
today. Those who accept Him will receive the new
birth, the indwelling Holy Spirit, and all the blessings
of salvation. Those who don't believe will render outward obedience; others will rebel and be punished by
death. But the essence of true faith will be inward
reality—not a mere outward compliance to Christ's
laws.

During the millennial age regenerated people will
control society. Therefore, all the beautiful and tender
elements of life will be much in evidence. The prophet
Jeremiah declared that in the towns of Judah and
streets of Jerusalem, places deserted during the great
tribulation, there "will be heard once more the sounds
of joy and gladness, the voices of bride and bridegroom,
and the voices of those who bring thank offerings to the
house of the Lord, saying, 'Give thanks to the Lord
Almighty, for the Lord is good; His love endures forever'" (Jeremiah 33:10,11).

The aged will be treated with respect, and little children will laugh and frolic without fear.

*This is what the Lord Almighty says: "Once again men*
*and women of ripe old age will sit in the streets of*
*Jerusalem, each with cane in hand because of his age.*
*The city streets will be filled with boys and girls playing*
*there" (Zechariah 8:4,5).*

In summary, under the blessings of the new covenant,
Israelites and Gentiles will enter the millennial age
with renewed hearts and a fresh awareness of the Holy
Spirit's presence in their lives. They and all who are
born again in subsequent generations will worship and
serve the Lord from their hearts in gratitude for His
mercies. The results of this inner transformation will
be apparent at every level of society.

*Universal Worship.* Second, in the millennial kingdom God will be worshiped by people everywhere, just
as He is today. The main difference is that a far larger

percentage of mankind will do so. The prophet Malachi, as God's spokesman, declared:

*"My name will be great among the nations, from the rising to the setting of the sun. In every place incense and pure offerings will be brought to My name, because My name will be great among the nations," says the Lord Almighty (Malachi 1:11).*

This prophecy does not contradict the idea that a new temple in Jerusalem will be the worship center of mankind. That such a temple will be built was clearly stated by Haggai. He was addressing a group of older Jewish people who were weeping because the temple built by Zerubbabel after the exile was far inferior to the one constructed by Solomon.

*This is what the Lord Almighty says: "In a little while I will once more shake the heavens and the earth, the sea, and the dry land. I will shake all nations, and the desired of all nations will come, and I will fill this house with glory," says the Lord Almighty. "The silver is Mine and the gold is Mine," declares the Lord Almighty. "The glory of this present house will be greater than the glory of the former house," says the Lord Almighty. "And in this place I will grant peace," declares the Lord Almighty (Haggai 2:6-9).*

In the last eight chapters of his book, the prophet Ezekiel gave us the details concerning this temple—its design and ritual. Its dimensions will be quite different from those of Israel's past. Besides, it will have no ark of the covenant, no lampstand, no table of showbread, and no veil between the holy place and the holy of holies. Jesus Christ has fulfilled everything to which they pointed. Moreover, His personal presence there will make all of these elements unnecessary.

Representatives from all nations will travel to Jerusalem so that they may worship there. They will "go up year after year to worship the King, the Lord Almighty, and to celebrate the Feast of Tabernacles" (Zechariah 14:16). The Lord said, "From one New Moon to another and from one Sabbath to another, all mankind will come and bow before Me" (Isaiah 66:23).

Men and women from all parts of the world (not necessarily every individual) will travel to Jerusalem to worship in this holy temple. In addition, according to Malachi, God will be worshiped by people everywhere, right where they are living!

*Memorial Sacrifices.* The sacrifices, which some see as a problem, are going to commemorate Christ's death on the cross. During the Old Testament era they pointed forward to Calvary. Now, in the church age, the Lord's Supper points back to the cross, and water baptism speaks of our identification with Christ in His death, burial, and resurrection. In the millennium, sacrifices will be offered at the temple as reminders of what Jesus Christ did through His offering of Himself on the cross.

This should not be thought strange. Horatius Bonar, a man highly revered for his saintliness and good sense, wrote:

> Why should not the *temple,* the *worship,* the *rites,* the *sacrifices,* be allowed to point to the Lamb that was slain, in the millennial age, if such be the purpose of the Father.... And if God should have yet a wider circle of truth to open up to us out of His Word concerning His Son, why should He not construct a new apparatus for the illustration of that truth? (Quoted by John L. Mitchell in *Bibliotheca Sacra,* July 1953, p. 267).

In conclusion, the kingdom age will feature a perfect priest-king in the person of Jesus Christ. He will head an effective government which will bring peace, prosperity, and righteousness to all mankind. Israel will be God's central nation and Jerusalem the world capital. Nature will be far more friendly to man and beast than it is today. And everything that is tender and beautiful in life will be honored and extolled.

The millennium will be the golden era of the "renewal of all things" (Matthew 19:28), the "times of refreshing ... from the Lord" (Acts 3:19), and the culmination of God's plan for our fallen earth. Therefore, let us pick up the chant of the Old Testament temple worshipers as they expressed their joyous anticipation of Messiah's coming to rule:

> *Let the heavens rejoice, let the earth be glad; let them say among the nations, "The Lord reigns!" Let the sea resound, and all that is in it; let the fields be jubilant, and everything in them! Then the trees of the forest will sing, they will sing for joy before the Lord, for He comes to judge the earth (1 Chronicles 16:31-33).*

# 12. The Binding and Releasing of Satan

All orthodox believers recognize the truth that Satan is a personal being. Moreover, we all agree that he was once a mighty angel who instigated and led a rebellion against God. The prophetic Scriptures also tell us about his binding, his brief release, and his ultimate consignment to the lake of fire.

The Scriptures do not give us a detailed description of Satan's revolt. Many biblical scholars believe, however, that it is alluded to in Isaiah 14:12-14 and Ezekiel 28:12-15. True, these prophecies are directed to the kings of Babylon and Tyre, but some of their pronouncements seem to go beyond a mere wicked earthling to a greater evil being behind the scenes. For example, in Isaiah 14:12 we read, "How you have fallen from heaven, O morning star, son of the dawn! You have been cast down to the earth, you who once laid low the nations!" And why would the king of Babylon be called "morning star, son of the dawn"? Could it be said of him that he had "fallen from heaven"? And in Eze-

kiel's lament concerning the king of Tyre, the prophet
wrote, "You were the model of perfection, full of
wisdom and perfect in beauty. You were in Eden, the
garden of God" (Ezekiel 28:12,13). These words certainly seem more applicable to a fallen angel than to an
earthly monarch.

Whether or not these words refer to the original fall
of Satan is open to debate, but the fact that a mighty
angel led a large number of his cohorts in a revolt
against God is a basic truth of the Bible. Some of the
devil's followers are now imprisoned in a place the
Scriptures call Tartarus (2 Peter 2:4; Jude 1:6). Many
of them live in an area called "the heavenly realms,"
and they are organized into a military-like hierarchy.
Paul wrote:

> For our struggle is not against flesh and blood, but
> against the rulers, against the authorities, against the
> powers of this dark world, and against the spiritual
> forces of evil in the heavenly realms (Ephesians 6:12).

From this region the devil and his followers have
access to earth. Peter gave believers this solemn
warning: "Be self-controlled and alert. Your enemy the
devil prowls around like a roaring lion looking for
someone to devour" (1 Peter 5:8).

A study of the Old Testament shows us that Satan's
method of working is not much different today than it
was during the centuries before Christ. While Jesus
was on earth, however, the devil and his followers in-
tensified their activities. They apparently realized
that He had come into the world to defeat them and to
provide redemption for mankind. They therefore
launched a full scale assault against the Lord Jesus.
But He overcame every temptation to sin. He revealed
His authority over demons by casting them out of
people they had possessed. He did not let the satanical-
ly induced hatred and treachery of the multitudes, the
Jewish leaders, or Judas Iscariot deter Him from going
to the cross to pay the price for man's redemption.
When our Lord gave up His spirit at Calvary, He sealed
the eventual doom of the devil and all his followers.

Our Lord's sinless life and atoning death made His resurrection inevitable. Because Jesus fought and won this decisive battle at Calvary, the writer of Hebrews declared:

> *Since the children have flesh and blood, he too shared in their humanity so that by His death He might destroy him who holds the power of death—that is, the devil—and free those who all their lives were held in slavery by their fear of death (Hebrews 2:14,15).*

Satan is still the "god of this age." He commands a large following of fallen angels and he actively opposes God and His people. But he does so with the realization of his ultimate doom. The crucial battle was fought during our Lord's earthly ministry, and it culminated at the cross. Jesus won the victory at Calvary.

With this background in mind, let's consider the future binding and releasing of Satan as it is described in Revelation 20:1-3, 7-10.

## THE BINDING OF SATAN

In a vision, John saw an angel come down from heaven with a key and a chain. The angel seized Satan, bound him, threw him into the abyss, locked it, and sealed it.

> *And I saw an angel coming down out of heaven, having the key to the Abyss and holding in his hand a great chain. He seized the dragon, that ancient serpent, who is the devil, or Satan, and bound him for a thousand years. He threw him into the Abyss, and locked and sealed it over him, to keep him from deceiving the nations any more until the thousand years were ended. After that, he must be set free for a short time (Revelation 20:1-3).*

When I was young, I was taught that the 1,000 years of Revelation 20 symbolized the entire church age. I was told that Satan is bound right now. I found this teaching somewhat confusing, because I knew that 1 Peter 5:8 declares that the devil is loose and prowling like a lion. But my pastor, a man for whom I still have great respect, assured me that Satan was bound, in the sense that he cannot now deceive the nations as he did during

Old Testament ages. He pointed out that Satan cannot keep the gospel from going out everywhere through personal witness, missionary activity, radio broadcasts, and literature. People in every country all over the world are turning to Jesus Christ for salvation. I accepted his explanation quite readily, but I somehow felt uneasy about it. It didn't square with what I read in the Bible. When somebody who didn't agree with this view rather humorously suggested that the devil must be on a very long leash, or on one made of rubber, I didn't know how to answer him. I had to admit that Revelation 20:1-3 portrays him as bound with a great chain and imprisoned in the abyss.

I know the arguments of those who think of Satan as bound today. Yes, they are right when they say that this passage contains some symbolism. The devil is not a flesh, blood, and bone creature who can be bound with a forged metal chain. The abyss very likely does not have an actual door that must be opened with a key wielded by an angel. But the meaning of the symbolism is clear enough: the devil will be thrown into the abyss and will remain there a prisoner for 1,000 years.

I am convinced that Satan will be bound during the millennium. This will give mankind a wonderful opportunity to obey God and enjoy a good life. Everyone will live under extremely prosperous and pleasant conditions, free from the deceptive work of Satan.

## THE RELEASE OF SATAN

At the close of the 1,000 years, the devil will be released from the abyss, gather a host of followers, and launch an attack on the city of Jerusalem.

> *When the thousand years are over, Satan will be released from his prison and will go out to deceive the nations in the four corners of the earth—Gog and Magog—to gather them for battle. In number they are like the sand on the seashore. They marched across the breadth of the earth and surrounded the camp of God's people, the city He loves. But fire came down from heaven and devoured them. And the devil, who*

*deceived them, was thrown into the lake of burning*
*sulphur, where the beast and the false prophet had been*
*thrown. They will be tormented day and night for ever*
*and ever (Revelation 20:7-10).*

The fact that Satan will be able to muster an army described as "like the sand of the seashore" in number is a striking declaration of human depravity. Think of it! Only saved people will have entered the millennium. All the salvation blessings and spiritual riches associated with the coming of the Holy Spirit on the Day of Pentecost will be theirs. They will live under the righteous rule of Jesus Christ in a beautiful, friendly, and comfortable environment. They will not suffer or die unless they deliberately disobey the Lord. They will not be subject to temptations from Satan. They will bring children into the world, and they will undoubtedly teach them the truths of God and try to influence them to receive Jesus Christ as their Savior. But they will not always be successful. As new generations of people come on the scene, many among them will obey the Lord Jesus only because they are afraid to do otherwise. They may attend worship services, but they will hate every minute of it. The number of these quiet rebels will multiply generation by generation, not because of satanic delusion, but because of their own inner depravity. We don't need the help of the devil to be selfish, immoral, cruel, proud, and stubborn. Jesus said:

*What comes out of a man is what makes him "unclean."*
*For from within, out of men's hearts, come evil*
*thoughts, sexual immorality, theft, murder, adultery,*
*greed, malice, deceit, lewdness, envy, slander,*
*arrogance and folly. All these evils come from inside*
*and make a man "unclean" (Mark 7:20-23).*

Oh, the depths of human depravity! Because sin entered the human family, all of us at heart are rebels. That's why Jesus declared, "I tell you the truth, unless a man is born again, he cannot see the kingdom of God" (John 3:3).

This great army of rebels, who join Satan at his

release, will make a move to capture Jerusalem. But the battle will never take place. Before the fighting begins, fire from heaven will kill every member of that assembled throng. The devil will be thrown into the "lake of burning sulphur," where he will join Antichrist and the false prophet, who will have been there for 1,000 years. They will remain in that dreadful place forever.

In summary, Satan will be bound by God for 1,000 years. He will be unable to deceive the citizens of the millennial kingdom. They will live in beautiful natural conditions and be at peace under the righteous rule of Christ. Yet many of them will rebel against the Lord Jesus. Those who do so openly will be severely punished. They will be shattered "to pieces like pottery" (Psalm 2:9), and slain "with the breath of His lips" (Isaiah 11:4). As a result, most of the unbelieving will not rebel openly. They will go through the motions of obedience while seething inwardly at their restrictions. They will endure conformity to Christ's rules like the skidrow derelict does the preaching service which precedes a free meal in a rescue mission. They will long for the day when they dare to rebel.

These rebels will receive their opportunity after the 1,000 years have passed, for God will not take away any person's freedom of choice. After Satan is released, he will convince the unsaved millennial citizens that they have a good chance of winning the battle against God. They will join his armies, but their revolt will come to a sudden end when fire falls from heaven and destroys them.

# 13. The Great White Throne

Final world destruction! Judgment day! These coming events belong together, and they are staggering to contemplate. Here is the apostle John's inspired portrait of them:

> Then I saw a great white throne and Him who was seated on it. Earth and sky fled from His presence, and there was no place for them. And I saw the dead, great and small, standing before the throne, and the books were opened (Revelation 20:11,12).

Seated on a luminous white throne in heaven will be One so glorious that earth and sky will seem to flee from His presence. Our planetary system will melt away and disappear just before He sits in judgment at the "great white throne." Hebrews 12:26-28 refers to it as a final shaking of our material universe that will bring about the removal of created things "so that what cannot be shaken may remain." The prophet Isaiah described the end of our present world as follows: "All the stars of the heavens will be dissolved and the sky rolled up like a scroll; all the starry hosts will fall like withered leaves from the vine, like shriveled figs from the fig tree" (Isaiah 34:4). Later he said, "The heavens will vanish like smoke" (Isaiah 51:6). The apostle Peter wrote, "The heavens will disappear with a roar; the elements will be destroyed by fire, and the earth and everything in it will be laid bare" (2 Peter 3:10).

This awesome dissolution of our present earth-system will be preceded by the translation of living believers and a resurrection of the dead. The people translated, in an event that is reminiscent of the rapture of the church, will be the millennial saints still alive when the thousand years are ended. The people resurrected will be all the dead who did not participate in the first resurrection.

This translation of the millennial saints is not described in the Bible, but I believe it will take place. In their earthly bodies they could not live through the terrific atomic-like explosion that will burn up our planetary-system. God could, of course, remove them from the earthly scene and preserve them in their flesh-and-blood bodies. But the present house in which our human spirit lives was never intended to be our eternal habitation. In 1 Corinthians 15:44 through 47 it is described as "natural" and as being "of the dust of the earth." The resurrection body, on the other hand, will be "spiritual."

The post-millennial resurrection will involve the lost of all the ages.

> The sea gave up the dead that were in it, and death
> and Hades gave up the dead that were in them
> (Revelation 20:13).

This verse states the all-inclusive extent of the resurrection. It will even include bodies that are buried in the sea. Some have said that these remains present a special problem because they will have disintegrated and become part of everything under the water. Even so, the Bible says they will be resurrected.

The statement that "death and Hades gave up the dead which were in them" perhaps refers to *body* and *soul.* The word "death" relates to the physical remains, whether decomposed in the ground, disintegrated in water, or burned by fire. "Hades" is the antechamber of hell where the souls of the wicked go at death. Every soul will leave that chamber, become embodied, and stand at the great white throne for judgment.

In this chapter we will take sufficient time to discuss quite thoroughly the great white throne judgment. We will consider the various elements that make up the total picture—the Judge, the subjects, the question, and the outcome.

## THE JUDGE

The Judge who will be seated on the great white throne will be Jesus Christ. John did not name Him, but it wasn't necessary for him to do so. Jesus Himself told us that He is going to be every person's final Judge, for He said, " . . . the Father judges no one, but has entrusted all judgment to the Son" (John 5:22). Paul declared the same truth to the Greek philosophers on Mars Hill by saying:

> For He [God] has set a day when He will judge the world with justice by the man He has appointed. He has given proof of this to all men by raising Him from the dead (Acts 17:31).

The majesty and holiness of Jesus Christ are revealed in the size and color of the throne—it is *great,* and it is *pure white.* The earth, which has been polluted by the iniquity of the human race (as climaxed in mankind's rejection and crucifixion of Jesus Christ), will flee from the presence of our Lord's purity and power. The sky, which represents the "heavenly regions" that have been defiled by harboring the fallen angels, will also disappear. Erich Sauer says, ". . . every scene of sin is dissolved." Jesus Christ will be the one perfect Judge of all history. His qualifications: absolute holiness, omniscience, omnipotence, and a firsthand knowledge of human problems.

## THE SUBJECTS

The subjects of the judgment will be "the dead, great and small" (Revelation 20:12). Just before our planetary system melts away, every person who did not participate in the "first resurrection" will be raised and transported to the great white throne.

This company will include, first of all, every unsaved person — the lost of the Old Testament era, the church age, the great tribulation, and the millennium. Jesus taught that the lost will be resurrected as well as the saved when He said, "Do not be amazed at this, for a time is coming when all who are in their graves will hear His voice and come out — those who have done good will rise to live, and those who have done evil will rise to be condemned" (John 5:28,29). This resurrection of the wicked will be "to shame and everlasting contempt" (Daniel 12:2). The voice of the Son of God will awaken the "sleeping" bodies of the unsaved, and they will stand before Him in judgment.

The second company at the great white throne will be the raptured millennial saints. Again, they aren't specifically mentioned, but we can assume that they will be there. You see, according to Hebrews 9:27, every person has this inevitable appointment with Christ. Why shouldn't they appear at the great white throne? It is doubtful that John would have mentioned the "book of life" if no saved people are going to stand there. As Erich Sauer has pointed out, Revelation 20:15 does not say, "Because *no one* was found written in the book of life, they will *all* be cast into the lake of fire." It reads, "*If anyone's* name was not found written in the book of life, he was thrown into the lake of fire."

## THE QUESTION

The issue at the great white throne will not be to decide a person's eternal destiny. Choosing between heaven or hell is always settled in this life. All final judgment in the presence of Christ relates to degrees of glory in heaven or of punishment in hell. At the great white throne the books that contain the divine record of human deeds will be opened. Each person will be judged according to what is written in them. Of course, Christ won't find it necessary to examine literal documents, because He is all-knowing. The symbolism of the books being opened teaches us that He will examine each life, taking into consideration all the factors. He will be aware of the time, talents, opportunities, and motives of each person before Him. People who did not have the written Word of God will not be held responsible for what they did not know. Paul told us, "All who sin apart from the law will also perish apart from the law, and all who sin under the law will be judged by the law" (Romans 2:12). The Lord will be absolutely impartial and just in rewarding the saved and in punishing the lost.

## THE OUTCOME

After this judgment, the millennial saints in their glorified bodies will join the rest of God's people in heaven. They will take their places with the believers of all preceding ages, each one shining with his own degree of glory.

The lost will go into the "lake of fire." We must not think of this place as a region filled with people writhing and screaming in pain. This would not allow room for our Lord's teaching about degrees of punishment. He said that it would be easier for the inhabitants of Sodom and Gomorrah and Tyre and Sidon than for people who had rejected Him and His message (Matthew 10:15; 11:21,22). He also declared, "That servant who knows his master's will and does not get ready or does not do what his master wants will be beaten with many blows. But the one who does not know and does things deserving punishment will be beaten with few blows" (Luke 12:47,48).

It is futile for us to speculate about the temperature in hell or the nature of the suffering that people will endure there. It will be God's penitentiary, and there He will dispense justice to each lost individual. Because He is perfectly holy, He must punish all disobedience. But His holiness also demands that He do so with absolute equity. In presenting the biblical doctrine of eternal punishment, we must neither minimize its severity nor exaggerate its intensity.

I don't like the idea of anyone suffering forever, not even the devil. I have often wished I could find one Bible statement that would give me a basis to say that every fallen angel and every human being will ultimately be saved. But not one passage even hints in that direction. Therefore, I must accept the doctrine of eternal punishment for the lost.

A profound sense of mystery should grip us as we contemplate the great white throne judgment and the eternal state of those who die unsaved. The picture of hell is grim: ". . . weeping and gnashing of teeth" (Matthew 22:13); ". . . their worm does not die, and the fire is not quenched" (Mark 9:48); ". . . trouble and distress" (Romans 2:9); ". . . the smoke of their torment rises for ever and ever" (Revelation 14:11). The frightening portrayal of these passages is lightened somewhat when we realize that they refer to people who had willfully, wantonly, and defiantly rejected God and set themselves to do evil.

Multitudes live and die, however, without ever hearing the gospel of salvation. Many of them endure suffering and pain from the cradle to the grave. Some people, especially those who are born in big city slums, never even see a trace of God's goodness and beauty in nature. They are sinners, and they all have a measure of responsibility. But they had so little light, so little opportunity. Therefore, I cannot imagine them enduring deep eternal anguish. I'm glad their final judgment and eternal punishment rests in the hands of Jesus Christ. Abraham asked the rhetorical question, "Will not the Judge of all the earth do right?" (Genesis 18:25). That comforts me! I also find great satisfaction in contemplating Paul's exclamation:

*Oh, the depth of the riches of the wisdom and knowledge of God! How unsearchable His judgments, and His paths beyond tracing out!*

*"Who has known the mind of the Lord? Or who has been His counselor?"*

*"Who has ever given to God, that God should repay him?"*

*For from Him and through Him and to Him are all things. To Him be the glory forever! Amen* (Romans 11:33-36).

# 14. The Glorious New World

As I sit here reflecting upon Revelation 21 and 22, my mind keeps going back to a conversation I had with an elderly husband and wife. Both were in very poor health and expected to die soon. As we talked about heaven, we agreed that it will be so different from earth that we can't form a clear mental picture of it. We discussed the fact that we can't even comprehend the nature of the resurrection body. All we know is that we will receive new bodies like the one Jesus has today. We are told that after He came from the grave, our Lord partook of food and invited people to touch Him. At the same time, however, He was able to pass through the walls of a closed room. Before I left this elderly couple, we agreed that many of our questions about eternity will not be answered until we leave this veil of tears and enter heaven's gates.

I've often tried to visualize the new Jerusalem as it is depicted in the last two chapters of Revelation. I can picture some of the physical details of the eternal city—its jewel-studded foundations, its clear jasper

wall, its pearly gates, and its golden streets. I can also
envision the sparkling radiance of the light of God shining through its walls of jasper and buildings of transparent gold. In my mind's eye I can see the crystal river
and the trees that will grow along its banks. But deep
within, I realize that the images I form in my mind are
earthly, not heavenly. From what the Bible tells me,
I know that this new world will be far different from
anything I have yet seen or experienced. I'm quite sure
that the second law of thermodynamics and the force of
gravity will not be operative there. I have an idea that
we will be able to travel at the speed of sound—perhaps
even faster than that. I'm not a disciple of the Greek
philosopher Plato, but I agree with the concept that
everything beautiful on earth is but a faint reflection
of a far more glorious counterpart in heaven.

I trust you will keep this truth in mind as you read
this chapter. The reality of heaven will be far more
beautiful than any word picture we can create on these
pages.

## THE NEW HEAVENS AND NEW EARTH

Revelation 21 opens with the words, "Then I saw a new
heaven and a new earth, for the first heaven and the
first earth had passed away." The "new heaven" mentioned here does not include paradise, the place where
God dwells, because that region has not been tainted by
sin. The "new heaven" relates to earth's solar system.
Along with our planet, it is going to be burned up,
melted away, and then re-created.

Some scholars insist that the new heaven and earth
will be a brandnew creation, not a renovation of our
present solar system. Others declare with equal conviction that the word "new" in Revelation 21:1 suggests
fresh life arising out of the decay and wreck of the old
world. At first sight, it seems as if these scholars are in
sharp disagreement, but closer analysis makes it clear
that the difference is mostly a matter of emphasis.

All Bible scholars agree that the new world will not
be a slightly reworked version of our present planetary

system. Some simply place more emphasis than others on the idea that the new heaven and new earth will arise out of the melted material of the old. The new world will not be created *ex nihilo* (out of nothing) as the universe was in the beginning. It will be drawn from or built upon the basic elements of our present solar system. No disagreement is found on this point.

Erich Sauer described the relationship between the old and new as follows:

> The coming earth is not "another" but a "new" one. Otherwise it could not be called a "new *earth.*" No, if John sees a new "heaven" and a new "earth," this proves that even in eternity the distinction between our planet and the heavenly places will in some fashion continue. With all transformation and transfiguration, even in that perfecting, the new plan of the universe will in some way correspond to the old.
>
> Doubtless the *material* also will be built in, even if in a manner still completely incomprehensible to us at present. God does not forsake the work of His hands. Furthermore, He will never give over His glorious material to Satan, His arch-enemy, to possess and destroy. With the new creation of heaven and earth it is very similar to the new creation of the individual soul. In Christ the individual is "a new creature; the old is gone; behold, all is become new" (2 Corinthians 5:17). And yet it is the same man with the same ego and the same soul. He has become new (cf. Revelation 21:4,5). Thus will God burn with fire His universal material, resolve it into its basic elements, split its atoms, free it from all restrictions, transform all things, and thus He will build the stones of the old structure into the new one according to a new plan. It is as if a piece of dirty coal were shut in a retort, by great heat made fluid as gas, and then afterward crystallized again into a glorious diamond. Thus God will not annihiliate but "change" (Psalm 102:26), not reject but redeem, not destroy but set in order, not abolish but create anew,

not ruin but transfigure (*The Triumph of the
Crucified,* Erich Sauer, Eerdmans, 1952,
pp. 178, 179).

## THE NEW JERUSALEM

After calling our attention to the new heaven and new
earth, John described a beautiful city that he saw descending from above and resting upon the new earth.

> *I saw the Holy City, the new Jerusalem, coming down
> out of heaven from God, prepared as a bride beautifully
> dressed for her husband. And I heard a loud voice from
> the throne saying, "Now the dwelling of God is with
> men, and He will live with them. They will be His
> people, and God Himself will be with them and be their
> God" (Revelation 21:2,3).*

This city will not be created after the renovation of our
present earth-system; rather, it exists today as the
"heavenly Jerusalem" (Hebrews 12:22). Right now it
is the place of God's core presence; the home of all the
redeemed who have died, and the abode of myriads of
angels. Some Bible scholars believe that it will be a
satellite city visible to earth-dwellers during the interval between the rapture and the end of the millennium.
Revelation 13:6 tells us that during the great tribulation the political world ruler will open "his mouth to
blaspheme God, and to slander His name and His dwelling place and those who live in heaven." In any case,
the heavenly city will come down from above and rest
upon the new earth. From this point on, it will be called
"the new Jerusalem."

The apostle John gave us the dimensions of this city.
He also described its jeweled foundations, its jasper
wall, its pearly gates, its golden streets, its crystal
river, its nourishing and health-giving trees, and its
glorious exclusions. We will consider each of these aspects of the new Jerusalem more closely.

*Its Dimensions.* Under the inspiration of the Holy
Spirit, the apostle depicted the new Jerusalem as being
far larger than any city in human history.

> *The angel who talked with me had a measuring rod*

*of gold to measure the city, its gates, and its wall. The*
*city was laid out like a square, as long as it was wide. He*
*measured the city with the rod and found it to be 12,000*
*stadia in length, and as wide and high as it is long*
*(Revelation 21:15,16).*

If we take these measurements literally, we must imagine a city almost 1500 miles in length, width, and height. At its base, a city like this in the United States would reach west from the shores of the Atlantic Ocean all the way to Denver; and from the northern edge of Maine to the southern tip of Florida. Such a huge and high city could not stand on our earth as it exists today, but the new earth will undoubtedly be far larger.

The fact that the city will be as high as it is long and wide has led to a great deal of discussion. Fifteen hundred miles is a long way up! Scholars who believe this description should be taken literally are divided as to whether the city will be in the form of a cube or a pyramid. If it is cubic, it will resemble a huge building with many floor levels—something difficult to envision. If it's pyramidal, it will be very steeply sloped to reach such a great height.

While I do not deny the possibility that the city could be shaped like a cube or pyramid as described above, I'm not sure we need to view it in either of these forms. Good reasons can be given for taking the position that the numbers and the other dimensional details are symbolic expressions. Erich Sauer has written:

But the numbers are not to be taken literally. What matters is the colossal vastness and the symbolic meaning of the sacred number twelve. Even while holding firmly the *embodiment* of spirit, it must be said that the figurative mirror of the eternal is by no means the same as the essence and content of the eternal. John himself testifies that the measure which the angel has is a human measure (Revelation 21:17), that is, that the angel employed human measures and forms, so as to bring the infinite to the consciousness of the finite spirit. He spoke to him in pictures of human conception, but the eternal itself is inconceivable, beyond our perception, super-earthly, super-worldly, simply "the other." The reality of its substance is therefore far from denoting the verbal literality of its measurements. The form in which its spirit embodiment is presented is figurative, the spirit embodiment itself is actual. The revelation therefore does not claim to give a description but only a hint of the eternal; what matters is not the form but that which forms it; the meaning is the ultimate, not its symbol. . . .

The ruling basic number is twelve: twelve foundations, twelve precious stones, twelve names of the apostles, twelve gates, twelve angels, twelve inscriptions on the gates, 12 times 12 the height of the wall, 12,000 furlongs the extent of the city on all sides (*The Triumph of the Crucified,* Erich Sauer, Eerdmans, 1952, pp. 193, 194).

This comment makes good sense, and it is consistent with other Bible passages that depict eternal or heavenly realities through visible representations. For example, in Ezekiel 1 the cherubim in heaven are described as having four wings and four faces, but in Revelation 4 they are portrayed with six wings and one face. This seems like a contradiction until we realize that these details are not to be interpreted literally. No creatures in heaven look like either of these portrayals. A being with four or six wings, beastlike legs, and a variety of faces—man, lion, ox, and eagle—would be a monstrosity. These details were not intended to be taken literally; rather, they represent spiritual truths about the cherubim. They are apparently angels of some kind who serve as instruments of God's government. The wings symbolize their swiftness to do His will. The four faces symbolize: intelligence, man; majesty, lion; patient service, ox; and keen discernment, eagle.

Similarly, the portrait of the glorified Christ in Revelation 1 is to be taken symbolically. Jesus doesn't look like an old man with white hair. He doesn't have eyes that blaze with fire, feet that look like burning bronze, or a tongue that is shaped like a sharp, double-edged sword. These details are symbols of abiding truths about our glorified Lord.

In short, John's description of the new Jerusalem's shape and size tells us that it will be beautifully symmetrical and large enough to accommodate everyone. I prefer this interpretation to one that insists that the details be taken literally. Although this is a possibility, I do not believe that we are locked into this literalistic concept.

*Its Foundations, Walls, and Gates.* John depicted the new Jerusalem as coming down and resting upon 12 jewel-studded foundations, and surrounded by a jasper wall with 12 gates made of pearl. As we consider this picture, let's remember that he was using earthly imagery to portray a world that will far transcend anything we can conceive in our present state.

The 12 foundation stones around the city will be above ground and visible to all who approach it.

*The foundations of the city walls were decorated with every kind of precious stone. The first foundation was jasper, the second sapphire, the third chalcedony, the fourth emerald, the fifth sardonyx, the sixth carnelian, the seventh chrysolite, the eighth beryl, the ninth topaz, the tenth chrysoprase, the eleventh jacinth, and the twelfth amethyst (Revelation 21:19-21).*

Each of the foundation stones is embellished with a different kind of jewel, symbolizing the harmonious variety that will exist in heaven. Moreover, the names of the 12 apostles are written on these foundation stones. This probably means that the new city will be founded on the message they proclaimed as representatives of both the Old and New Testament saints. In their teaching and preaching they took great pains to point out that the life, death, burial, resurrection, ascension, and return of Jesus Christ were prophesied in the Old Testament. The eternal truths they proclaimed formed the foundation for the salvation of the redeemed in every age.

The wall of the city will be made of jasper and will measure about 216 feet in height.

*He measured its wall and it was 144 cubits thick, by man's measurement, which the angel was using. The wall was made of jasper (Revelation 21:17,18).*

While the *New International Version* says that the wall will be 144 cubits "thick," the margin indicates that this may refer to its height. A wall 216 feet high cannot be scaled by human effort. Only those who have come to God through Jesus Christ will be permitted into the heavenly city. The jasper walls are transparent; therefore, they allow the light from the city to shine outward in blessing upon the whole new earth. The "nations," probably the millennial saints, who inhabit the new earth will bask in the light of God's glory.

The gates are 12 in number, and each is made of a large pearl. Each gate is guarded by an angel and contains the name of one of Israel's 12 tribes.

*It had a great, high wall with twelve gates, and with twelve angels at the gates. On the gates were written the names of the twelve tribes of Israel. There were three gates on the east, three on the north, three on the south, and three on the west. The twelve gates were twelve pearls, each gate made of a single pearl (Revelation 21:12,13,21).*

Notice that the gates are open, and that an angel will stand at each of them. He will not be there to guard against enemy intruders, for the wicked will have been banished in the lake of fire. The angel at each open gate is a beautiful contrast to the picture with which Genesis 3 closes. There a cherubim with a drawn sword was placed as a guard to keep Adam and Eve from returning to Eden. Here the gate is wide open, and the angel is there to guarantee entrance, exit, and re-entrance for all the inhabitants of the new world.

The names of the 12 tribes of Israel, one on each gate, will be a reminder of the truth that salvation is from the Jews (John 4:22). The apostle Paul referred to Jesus Christ as the Son of God "who as to His human nature was a descendant of David" (Romans 1:3).

The gates being made of pearl may suggest the truth that our redemption was purchased through the suffering and death of Jesus Christ. As is well known, a pearl is formed inside the shell of an oyster. A strong fluid is secreted that protects the shellfish from a foreign particle that becomes lodged in the soft tissue.

*Its Transparent Gold.* The apostle John revealed that the buildings and streets of the new Jerusalem will be made of transparent gold.

*The wall was made of jasper, and the city of pure gold, as pure as glass.... The street of the city was of pure gold, like transparent glass (Revelation 21:18,21).*

Transparent gold doesn't exist today, but we can visualize what it would be like. The color reminds us of sunlight. The imagery suggests to me that God's light will reflect from the streets, shine through the buildings, and fill every inhabitant of the city with great joy.

*Its River and Trees.* The city will also have a crystal river and health-giving trees.

*Then the angel showed me the river of the water of life, as clear as crystal, flowing from the throne of God and of the Lamb down the middle of the great street of the city. On each side of the river stood the tree of life, bearing twelve crops of fruit, yielding its fruit every month. And the leaves of the tree are for the healing of the nations (Revelation 22:1,2).*

This passage is generally interpreted as saying that the river of life will run down the middle of an avenue, dividing it into two lanes like a boulevard. Trees will line each side of the crystal river. The well-known commentator Lenski, however, insists that this is not an accurate conception. Basing his idea on the meaning of the Greek word *poiamou,* he contends this is a picture of a beautiful park that will run through the entire city, with an avenue on one side and a river on the other. I'm not sure which view is more accurate, but it makes relatively little difference. What matters to me is that these verses give me the assurance that heaven will be a place of great natural beauty. The river will flow unceasingly for our joy and satisfaction. The trees which grow alongside it, a species called "the Tree of Life," will give fruit that will nourish us and bear leaves that will keep us well forever. In paradise we will experience fully the truth expressed by the psalmist, "They feast on the abundance of Your house; You give them drink from Your river of delights. For with You is the fountain of life; in Your light we see light" (Psalm 36:8,9).

*Its Glorious Exclusions.* Having considered the things that will constitute some of the glories of the heaven, let's now look at some of the things that will *not* be there. Nothing unpleasant will greet us when we enter our eternal home, nor will evil come in to mar our joy.

First, in the new heaven and new earth there will no longer be any sea (Revelation 21:1). Large bodies of water, so essential now for maintaining a proper oxygen level, won't be needed in heaven. The crystal river mentioned earlier will either empty into a subterranean pool or circle back to its source.

This declaration that the new earth will contain no sea was undoubtedly very comforting to the second-century Christians who read the book of Revelation. To them the sea represented forced separation, baffling mystery, as well as dangerous tempests. The prophet declared, "But the wicked are like the tossing sea, which cannot rest, whose waves cast up mire and mud" (Isaiah 57:20). The endtime political world leader of Revelation 13 will rise out of the sea, a picture of the unrest among the nations. The absence of the sea in the new heaven and new earth therefore symbolizes the end of all unfortunate geographical divisions, painful mysteries, fevered restlessness, and disturbing tumult.

The second glorious exclusion of the new heaven and earth consists of a package: "There will be no more death or mourning or crying or pain" (Revelation 21:4). The statement which precedes it, "He will wipe every tear from their eyes," is sometimes taken to

mean that God will comfort us after we weep at the
judgment seat of Christ. I personally do not believe this
is a correct interpretation of these words; rather, I view
them as telling us that tears will have no place in
heaven. Because no one will ever die in heaven, we will
never mourn as we do now when a loved one is taken
from us. We will never cry hot tears of frustration, because we will never experience disappointment or
failure. We will never shed tears of pain because no one
will ever be ill or injured.

The third item conspicuous by its absence in our
glorious new home will be a temple. John wrote, "I did
not see a temple in the city, because the Lord God Almighty and the Lamb are its temple" (Revelation
21:22). God designed the tabernacle and the temple as
earthly centers for real, though imperfect, worship.
But in glory we will worship Him perfectly because He
will dwell in the midst of His people. How wonderful is
this promise: "Now the dwelling of God is with men,
and He will live with them. They will be His people, and
God Himself will be with them and be their God"
(Revelation 21:3). Faith will then be turned to sight.

The fourth blessed absence in heaven has to do with
impure substances and wicked beings.

> *Nothing impure will ever enter it, nor will anyone who
> does what is shameful or deceitful, but only those whose
> names are written in the Lamb's book of life*
> *(Revelation 21:27).*

The new Jerusalem will be free from all physical,
moral, and spiritual impurity. No wicked individual,
human or angelic, will ever enter the new heaven and
new earth.

> *Outside are the dogs, those who practice magic arts, the
> sexually immoral, the murderers, the idolaters, and
> everyone who loves and practices falsehood*
> *(Revelation 22:15).*

The term "outside" does not mean that the wicked and
ungodly will be somewhere just outside the gates of the
new Jerusalem. They will be in the lake of fire, from
which they will never be released. We today live in the

midst of people who practice sorcery, live immorally, perpetrate violent crimes, seek gods of their own making, and practice deceit. No impure person or thing will be present in the new world to which we are going.

The fifth category of things absent from our heavenly home has to do with the sun and moon and night. It appears that when God dissolves our solar system He will bring to an end the present orbit of the earth around the sun as it turns upon its own axis.

*The city does not need the sun or the moon to shine on it, for the glory of God gives it light, and the Lamb is its lamp. The nations will walk by its light, and the kings of the earth will bring their splendor into it. On no day will its gates ever be shut, for there will be no night there. The glory and honor of the nations will be brought into it (Revelation 21:23-26).*

A light that has its source in God Himself will cover the whole earth. It will apparently shine without interruption, bringing to an end our present distinction between day and night. It is hard for us to conceive of a world in which time cannot be broken down into segments—seconds, minutes, hours, days, weeks, months, and years. Yet the Bible makes it clear that the present divisions in time will not exist in eternity. This does not mean, however, that we will be unaware of past, present, or future. A rational being can't live without memories, present activities, and plans. I believe we will have some way of measuring time in God's eternity, but we will be free from its tyranny. We will never run out of time because we will "have forever."

To summarize, the lovely and uplifting elements of our present life will be retained and augmented in the new world that awaits us. No evil and unpleasantness will be there. The jewel-studded foundations, jasper wall, pearly gates, and golden streets speak of a real world with a glory that far transcends anything we can visualize. When we draw a mental picture of a beautiful park with a crystal river on one side and a broad avenue on the other, let's remember that the reality in heaven will be far more lovely than anything we can portray. When we put together all the positive features along with the list of all the things that won't be there, we have only a faint glimpse of heaven. Let us await our glorious new home with joyous anticipation.

Think of it! We will see the Lord Jesus face-to-face! We will worship and serve our triune God exactly as we should! We will live with one another in perfect harmony! We will exercise authority over angels! And all of this will go on forever!

During the Middle Ages, Bernard of Cluny composed a poem that to me provides a fitting close for this book. It expresses the noble sentiments of a redeemed soul filled with wonder and awe and the contemplation of heaven's glory.

> Jerusalem the golden,
>   With milk and honey blest,
> Beneath thy contemplation
>   Sink heart and voice oppressed:
> I know not, O I know not,
>   What social joys are there,
> What radiancy of glory,
>   What light beyond compare!
>
> They stand, those halls of Zion,
>   Conjubilant with song,
> And bright with many an angel,
>   And all the martyr-throng;
> The Prince is ever in them,
>   The daylight is serene,
> The pastures of the blessed
>   Are decked in glorious sheen.
>
> The cross is all thy splendor,
>   The Crucified thy praise,
> His laud and benediction
>   Thy ransomed people raise:
> Jesus, the crown of beauty,
>   True God and Man, they sing,
> Their never-failing portion,
>   Their glorious Lord and King.

# *Scripture Index* 159